A PASTORAL LETTER

The Cry of the Earth
– *The Cry of the Poor*

THE CLIMATE CATASTROPHE – CREATION'S URGENT CALL FOR CHANGE

Archbishop Dermot Farrell

D1637690

VERITAS

Contents

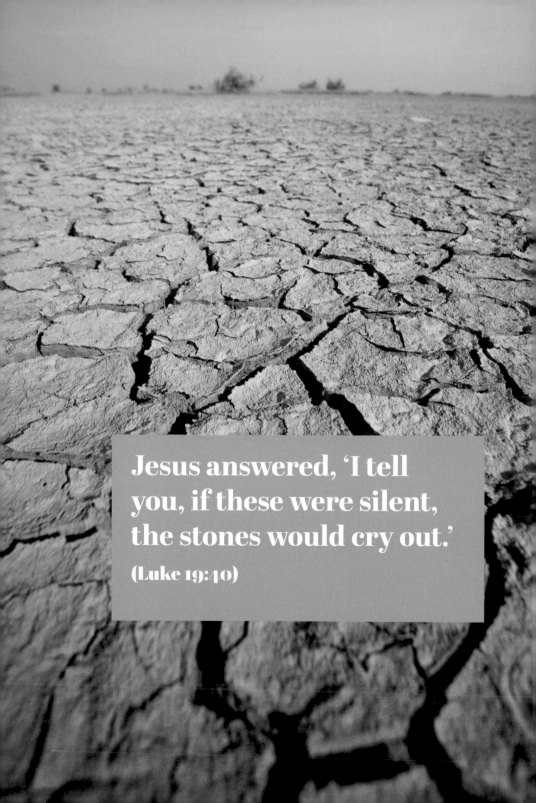

Jesus answered, 'I tell you, if these were silent, the stones would cry out.'

(Luke 19:40)

Introduction

'Which of these three', asked Jesus, 'was neighbour to the man who fell into the hands of the robbers?' (Luke 10:36) Our planet, our common home, has 'fallen into the hands of robbers who have stripped it' of its assets, and plundered it, 'and have gone away, leaving it half dead' (see Luke 10:30).

> We are squeezing the goods of the planet. Squeezing them, like an orange. ... Today, not tomorrow, today, we have to take care of Creation with responsibility.[1]

The parable of the Good Samaritan (Luke 10:25–37) is not some story about goodness, it is a parable about involvement. What sets the Samaritan apart is that he is someone who *acts*. He sees, he has compassion, he acts, he gets involved. For Jesus, he is the model of our response to the world: he becomes involved in the situation in which he finds himself. Our world is being plundered; we cannot walk away leaving it half dead.

In our age 'we are confronted with two interconnected crises: the coronavirus pandemic and the ecological crisis. Both require urgent action, but they also require a sense of purpose which comes from a clear vision.'[2] In this pastoral letter, I wish to reflect further on this theme so that we may enter our faith more deeply, respond more actively to the situation in which we find ourselves, and live our God-given lives more vibrantly. I do so in a spirit of engagement and dialogue, taking to heart what the Second Vatican Council said when – sixty years ago – it exhorted: 'We must recognise and understand the world in which we live, its vision of itself, its longings, and its often dramatic characteristics.'[3]

1. 'We are squeezing the goods of the planet. Squeezing them, like an orange. Countries and companies in the North have been enriched by exploiting natural gifts from the South, generating an "ecological debt". Who is going to pay that debt? Furthermore, the "ecological debt" is enlarged when multinationals do outside their countries what they are not allowed to do in their own. It is outrageous. Today, not tomorrow, today, we have to take care of Creation with responsibility. Let us pray that the goods of the planet are not plundered, but are shared in a fair and respectful way. No to plundering, yes to sharing.' Pope Francis, Video Message for the Month of Creation, 31 August 2020.
2. Archbishop Dermot Farrell, Address upon appointment as Archbishop of Dublin, 29 December 2020.
3. *Oportet itaque ut mundus in quo vivimus necnon eius exspectationes, appetitiones et indoles saepe dramatica cognoscantur et intelligantur.* Second Vatican Council, Pastoral Constitution on the Church in the Modern World, *Gaudium et Spes*, 7 December 1965, 4.

According to the most recent and very sobering UN Intergovernmental Panel on Climate Change (IPCC) report, climate change is rapid, extensive, and intensifying. The climate catastrophe is causing major climate disruption, which in many instances is irreversible.[4] This pastoral letter is not an attempt to replace either what scientists, civic leaders or various climate movements are saying. Neither does it seek to displace the appropriate leadership which is their responsibility. Consequently, the importance of the forthcoming UN Climate Change Conference of the Parties (COP26), which will take place in Glasgow from 31 October to 12 November 2021, is to be noted. Such conferences and their common agreements are vital in raising public awareness and creating political momentum in the face of the climate catastrophe. This pastoral letter seeks to engage a further dimension, and approaches the climate catastrophe from the conviction of faith: this means facing the crisis with a deep sense of reality and a profound sense of hope. 'Faith is not a light which scatters all our darkness, but a lamp which guides our steps in the night and suffices for the journey.'[5] It therefore means daring to look at the crisis from another perspective: the perspective of God. Looking at our planet from the perspective of the Creator permits us to see things from beyond, as it were.[6] This pastoral letter is addressed in a particular way to people of faith in the Archdiocese of Dublin. It is a word of encouragement and a call to action in the face of something that threatens every aspect of our lives today and into the future. It asks how we follow

---

4. The IPCC report (*Climate Change 2021: The Physical Science Basis*) was published on 9 August 2021, and widely reported upon.

5. 'Faith is not a light which scatters all our darkness, but a lamp which guides our steps in the night and suffices for the journey ... God does not provide arguments which explain everything; rather his response is that of an accompanying presence, a history of goodness which touches every story of suffering and opens up a ray of light' (Pope Francis, *Lumen Fidei*, 57). This pastoral is written in the spirit of the Second Vatican Council, and is motivated by 'the Christian convictions that inspire and sustain' the Church. See Pope Francis, *Fratelli Tutti*, 6.

6. This is where Job is brought when God speaks to him out of the whirlwind:

Where were you when I laid the foundation of the earth? Tell me, if you have understanding.

Who determined its measurements – surely you know! Or who stretched the line upon it?

On what were its bases sunk, or who laid its cornerstone

when the morning stars sang together and all the heavenly beings shouted for joy? (Job 38:4–7)

Jesus in this unprecedented crisis. How do we live our faith in this new time? How do we pray, and what difference does prayer make? What is God saying to the world? What is the Spirit saying to the churches? (see Rev 3:22). As your bishop, I wish to explore these and other questions with you.

Part of the difficulty in addressing the climate crisis is that its vastness and complexity blinds our day-to-day lives to the part we have to play in addressing it. 'Climate [is] an overarching, underlying condition of our lives and planet, and the change [that has led to this crisis – still unreal for so many –] was incremental and intricate and hard to recognize, [unless one was keeping] track [of its detail]. Climate catastrophe is a slow shattering of the stable patterns that governed the weather, the seasons, the species and migrations, [and] all the beautifully orchestrated systems of' this extraordinary planet which we share.[7] Paradoxically, for all of us in the developed world, our fear of the 'lifestyle cost' of acting for the common good induces a lethal paralysis. When we gain perspective and realise what is at stake for the future of our children and grandchildren, and what is already at stake for the vulnerable in the world's underdeveloped regions, we are empowered to act.[8] Without doubt this is a long-term undertaking. It foresees many perspective shifts – political, social, economic and ecclesial. While overwhelming at first, long-term societal change can occur; for example, the societal shift in attitudes towards smoking, or the shift away from fossil fuels, now gaining momentum.

The ensuing life-giving humility is a gift of the Holy Spirit, and part of the narrow door of which Jesus speaks (see Luke 13:24). It expresses itself in both prayer and action. While action is called for, prayer is as vital for the person of faith, as prayer both sustains the long journey, and permits the believer to discern the call of the Spirit, the Lord of Life (see Gen 1:2). See further, the sections on prayer below.

7. Rebecca Solnit, 'Our Climate Change Turning Point is Right Here, Right Now', *The Guardian*, 12 July 2021, www.theguardian.com/ commentisfree/2021/jul/12/our-climate-change-turning-point-is-right-here-right-now.

8. In the same article, Solnit perceptively observed that as well as threatening our future, climate chaos – as she terms the effects of climate change – threatens our past. While war, conflict and poverty have always devastated the cultures and history of those who lost, the effects of climate change destroy material culture and fragile environments. In this, climate change increases the impoverishment of all humanity. On the cultural impoverishment that frequently follows environmental degradation, see *Laudato Si'*, 143–6.

1. Our Rapidly Changing World

> Never has humanity had such power over itself, yet
> nothing ensures that it will be used wisely, particularly
> when we consider how it is currently being used.
>
> (Pope Francis, *Laudato Si'*, 104)

The events of the past eighteen months have brought home
to us that our planet and its social organisation is much more
fragile and complex than many of us previously realised. It is now
beyond doubt that our climate is changing in response to what we
as humans have done to upset its equilibrium. The average global
temperature is now 1.1 degrees Celsius above what it was during
the second half of the nineteenth century, and last year, 2020,
was the joint warmest year, with 2016, since temperature records
began. Though these changes in temperature might seem small,
they have knock-on effects in other areas of climate, and are
already seriously affecting the lives of people across the globe,
people with whom we share this planet, our common home.

1.1 Looking at Our World with the Eyes of Faith

Christian faith is rooted in the reality of the Incarnation. In the
Incarnation, God embraces humankind anew. Because we do not
live in a vacuum, but are part of this world, God in Christ also
embraces creation anew. When Christians speak of the world,
they speak of that through which God reveals himself and his
inner life.[9] The living faith of both Judaism and Christianity sees
creation as a witness to the love of God, and to the nature of the
Creator, who made us and calls us into life each day. As it says
in the psalm:

> The heavens proclaim the glory of God,
> and the firmament shows forth the work of his hands.
> Day unto day takes up the story
> and night unto night makes known the message.
> No speech, no word, no voice is heard

---

9. 'God, who through the Word creates all things (see John 1:3) and keeps them in existence, gives humanity an enduring witness to Himself in created realities (see Rom. 1:19-20).' Second Vatican Council, Dogmatic Constitution on Divine Revelation, *Dei Verbum*, 18 November 1965, 3.

yet their span extends through all the earth,
their words to the utmost bounds of the world.

(Psalm 19:2–5)[10]

'The world was made to communicate the glory of God,' St Bonaventure would later say, 'to help us to discover in its beauty the Lord of all, and to return to him.'[11]

Approaching the world from the conviction of faith is a call to hope. Christian hope is not an easy hope; easy hope is little more than a form of complacency. The hope that comes from faith is not a flight from disaster or danger, but the foundation of committed response and decisive action. The Christian does not fabricate hope, but hope comes from God who is its foundation.[12] Our faith is not a flight from the world, but faith provides (see Gen 22:14) a meaningful framework within which people can make decisions and take action.[13]

Such a stance is in sharp contrast to a utopian approach that is founded upon a world we don't have, and that takes flight from reality into a world that never was and can never be. I ask you to join with me in reflecting on the threat, posed by the climate crisis, to the existence of our world as we know it. More than that, I ask you to join with me in wondering what people of faith and communities of faith – the people and parishes of the Archdiocese of Dublin – might do to mitigate this disaster. I ask you to join with me in reading our world – the 'Book of Nature', as the ancients called it. Alongside the Book of Nature, I also ask you to join me in reading the Scriptures, the Word of God – the other great book of our faith – in a quest for insight, inspiration and strength so as to live in a new way on this earth, our common home. Nothing less is called for. The earth cries out to us. And God, the Lord of Life, calls us to embrace a new culture: a culture

10. 'Nature as a whole not only manifests God but is also a locus of God's presence. The Spirit of Life dwells in every living creature and calls us to enter into relationship with him.' *Laudato Si'*, 88, citing *The Church and the Ecological Question*, a declaration of the Brazilian Bishops from 1992 (*A Igreja e a Questão Ecológica* [São Paulo: Edições Paulinas, 1992], 53–4).

11. Pope Francis, Message for the World Day of Peace 2020, citing Saint Bonaventure *In II Sent.*, I, 2, 2, q. 1, conclusion and *Breviloquium*, II, 5.11.
12. See Pope Benedict XVI, *Spe Salvi*, 31.
13. This is what is found in another key in the Letter of James: 'Show me your faith apart from your works, and I by my works will show you my faith' (James 2:18). Faith without action is dead and unreal.

of care – for the earth and for each other, especially the poor, the invisible and those left behind.

In a prophetic act, Pope Francis published an encyclical letter in 2015 entitled, *Laudato Si': On the Care of our Common Home*. The first words, borrowed from St Francis of Assisi, set the tone:

> '*Laudato Si', mi' Signore*' – 'Praise be to you, my Lord'. ... [O]ur common home is like a sister with whom we share our life and a beautiful mother who opens her arms to embrace us. ... This sister now cries out to us because of the harm we have inflicted on her by our irresponsible use and abuse of the goods with which God has endowed her. We have come to see ourselves as her lords and masters, entitled to plunder her at will.　　　　(*LS*, 1–2)

Six years later – as the whole world negotiates the Covid-19 pandemic, the climate crisis and the threat to biodiversity – the call of *Laudato Si'* is not only still relevant but it is even more prophetic. Let us look briefly at what is happening to our common home and the part we play in that. Let us do so in an attempt to discover how we can live more sustainably, more responsibly, and more humanly in our common home. Tirades against progress, discourses built on guilt and baths of nostalgia are not constructive; they have little or nothing to contribute to the life-giving and life-enhancing gift that is the gospel of our Lord and Saviour. Cardinal José Tolentino Mendonça put it well: 'Wisdom is on the side of the announcers of hope and not on the apocalyptic preachers of tragedy.'[14]

2. The Effects of Climate Change: Four Inter-layered Crises

Climate change is not simply a crisis about climate; it is about far more than 'climate'. It may be best described as a 'serious socio-environmental crisis'.[15] The change in the world's climate has many effects, and all of these have serious consequences for the future of our world. We may single out four that capture

14. See *Thirst: Our Desire for God, God's Desire for Us* (New York: Paulist, 2019), 52. *Thirst* is the text of Cardinal Tolentino Mendonça's Lenten retreat to Pope Francis and the papal household in 2018.

15. See Pope Francis, Words of Greeting to the Global Catholic Climate Movement at the General Audience of 1 February 2017.

the character of the complex and far-reaching effects of climate change: the water crisis; the depletion of soil; the breakdown of biodiversity; increasing poverty and injustice. Looking at these effects will help us to take on board what Pope Saint John Paul II and Patriarch Bartholomew realised almost twenty years ago when, in 2002, they declared that the challenge the world faces 'is not simply economic and technological; it is moral and spiritual'.[16] Pope Benedict XVI continued this emphasis by drawing attention to the values of authentic or integral development, human ecology, and environmental degradation and sensitivity to the vulnerable and suffering in an era of economic globalisation and technological development. His encyclical, *Caritas in Veritate* (2009) showed how environmental degradation was related to disordered economic and political relationships, and was clear on the obligations of highly developed nations to act in solidarity with nations on the road to development.[17]

Climate change now means that the survival of our planet as we know it hangs in the balance. The reality that impinges upon us is so frightening that we fear even to consider it. We are in denial. We fear the consequences and the cost of thinking it through. Instead, we permit ourselves to be seduced by the illusion that, in the end, things will somehow work out, that some 'fantastic' all-embracing solution will be discovered.[18] This denial is nothing less than the doorway of death: death of nature's diversity, of its beauty and mystery, death of people driven from

16. Common Declaration on Environmental Ethics, 10 June 2002.
17. See Christiana Z. Peppard, 'Hydrology, Theology, and *Laudato Si*", *Theological Studies* 77 (2016): 416–35; here 419.
18. While the shift to electric vehicles is rightly flagged as a game-changer in automobility, it has to be borne in mind that the move to electric vehicles places new pressures on electricity distribution networks and reveals new vulnerabilities. Addressing such exposure demands long-term strategic solutions, often involving large governmental investment, and brings differing inter- governmental priorities, national vulnerabilities as well as the risks of opportunistic politics, and deep-seated international tensions. In an era of increasing nationalism and populism, stable outcomes for the common good become increasingly difficult to achieve. This is also noticeable in the different approaches to energy generation even across various countries in Europe: one sees significant differences in how fossil-fuelled power generation is to be replaced, whether only by renewables or whether nuclear power again becomes an acceptable option.

their homes and their lands by drought, floods, hunger, or raw economic necessity, death of the dreams we have for our children and our children's children.[19] This denial takes away our true freedom and puts us, our society and our culture in the stranglehold of exploitative patterns of power and manipulation, patterns which are as destructive as they are hidden. The earth cries out to us. We may think that the cry of the earth is about its need. It is – but it is about much more! May we hear in the cry of the earth its truth: the call to life for ourselves.

2.1 The Water Crisis[20]

There is no life without water. We cannot survive without it. Sometimes we call Planet Earth, the Blue Planet. Salt water accounts for 97.5 per cent of all water in the earth; the remaining 2.5 per cent is fresh water. This 2.5 per cent sustains human life on earth – our life. In a real sense it is the foundation of all human civilisation; however, because it seems to be in such abundance, we appear to take water for granted. While fresh water is a global concern, it is always a local issue.[21] Most people drink from the well in their own yard. In the past one hundred and fifty years, with the significant industrialisation of society and of agriculture, the demand for fresh water has increased exponentially, and the effects of vastly increased urban living can be seen in our rivers, lakes and oceans.

2.1.1 Rivers and Oceans Under Threat

In the 1980s, five hundred rivers in Ireland were considered to be 'pristine'; however, this number has now fallen to just twenty according to the Environmental Protection Agency. The reasons for this are complex, contributed to by industrial, agricultural and demographic factors. The effect is that complex ecosystems are damaged and even destroyed. This means both a loss of biodiversity and also the creation of unworthy and unhealthy

19. See further, *Querida Amazonia*, 14: '[W]hen local authorities give free access to the timber companies, mining or oil projects, and other businesses that raze the forests and pollute the environment, economic relationships are unduly altered and become an instrument of death.'

20. See further *Laudato Si'*, 27–31.
21. The use of the planet's 'fresh water' merits much reflection: 70 per cent is used in agriculture, 22 per cent goes to industrial uses, while the remaining 8 per cent is consumed in domestic settings: cooking, bathing, and cleaning.

environments for human living: we end up living in places that are far less healthy and far less beautiful than the world that God wants for us.

As an island nation, the deterioration of the oceans in recent times has an effect on us also. Without the oceans our planet would be as inhospitable as Mars: no meadows, no insects, no forests, no flowers, no birds, no animals and no humans. Today the oceans are under enormous attack from many different sources. To name some, one might look at the presence of plastics, the impact of commercial fishing and the surprising consequences of sub-aquatic noise pollution.

The media – both print and visual – have been filled with reports and images of the effect of plastic on ocean life. We have been shocked by images of huge whales no longer able to feed because of the plastic they have ingested. We have become aware of the ubiquitous presence of microplastic in all the oceans, how it makes its way into the food chain and into our bloodstream.[22] In contrast to other areas, the everyday choices we make (for example, in moving away from disposables) can over time address this problem in a real way.

In the twentieth century, fish catches have grown by a staggering twentyfold from 3 million metric tons at the beginning of the century to almost 90 million tons by the end of the century. This level of harvesting is not sustainable.

Few people realise that noise pollution from a variety of sources, such as the roar of ships' propellers and dynamite fishing, is causing huge damage to marine life. All the creatures of the sea use sound to navigate, find prey, defend territory and attract mates, so the present cacophony is very destructive.

Rising ocean levels, due to increased global warming, endanger many coastal city and island communities. Here in Ireland, we are already experiencing changes in our island that are likely to become more severe as time goes on. While it is not certain how drastic and how widespread these will be, they will impact on the lives of our young people with increasing severity. We are seeing more intense storms and rainfall events,

22. This is not of mere passing interest: there is no longer any place on earth free from microplastics. They have been found on the peak of Mount Everest, in the deepest trench of the ocean, and in our bloodstreams. Even the child in the womb is being infused with inorganic material. An unhealthy planet affects life at every level.

greater water shortages during summer droughts, increased river and coastal flooding, further deterioration of our water quality, changes in plant and animal species. Sea-level rises will certainly erode the soft Irish coastline and result in increased inundation in our many coastal cities and towns. It becomes clear that businesses, transport systems, farms, fisheries and our homes will have to respond to these changed conditions. This can only happen if our way of life changes in order to adapt to climate change, while our economy remains competitive and capable of sustaining future generations.

This requires a change of heart, as without a change from within, there will be no enduring change in lifestyle. As the Australian bishops put it almost a decade ago, 'We must examine our lives and acknowledge the ways in which we have harmed God's creation through our actions and our failure to act.'[23] This is part of what Pope Francis calls 'ecological conversion': shifting our gaze from ourselves to the world in need around us, from those closest to us to those furthest away.[24]

2.1.2 Water and Women: Water, Justice and Gender

Injustice around water does not affect all people equally. It is not just a contrast between the developed and developing worlds; the reality is that women and children are disproportionately impacted by poor access to clean water. Gender is a major factor in water and sanitation, for it is often women and girls who bear the burden of procuring water when it is scarce. Around the world, women and children spend an estimated 200 million hours *every single day* collecting water. In addition to danger and susceptibility to injury, children responsible for supplying water to their families are unable to attend school. When it comes to education, there is a direct link between access to clean water and attendance rates.[25] How can a child study or concentrate when she is exhausted from carrying water over long distances? Education has transformed our country

23. Australian Catholic Bishops' Conference, *A New Earth: The Environmental Challenge*, 2002. Cited in LS, 218.
24. See Pope Francis, *Laudato Si'*, 216–21, and the General Audience, Rome, 15 December 2015.

25. According to UNICEF, girls' enrolment rates increase by 15 per cent when they are provided with access to clean water.

and provided opportunities for a fuller life in successive generations. Should not all the children of the world have easy access to this gift?

Justice is not some vague hope for a better world. Justice demands action. The climate crisis will not be addressed globally until the globe becomes more equitable. We have to act in order that the burdens imposed on people because of their gender or status are more equitably distributed.

2.1.3 Light from God's Word

For the psalmist, God's Lordship and his creative power are made manifest by the immensity of the oceans. God's deepest gift is not water but the life and salvation that he bestows on all earth's creatures. As we hear the cry of the poor, let us call upon the Creator who caused a river to flow in Eden (see Gen 2:10) so that all could live in the garden of the world.[26]

> The Lord's voice resounding on the waters,
> the Lord on the immensity of waters;
> the voice of the Lord, full of power,
> the voice of the Lord, full of splendour.
> The Lord sat enthroned over the flood;
> the Lord sits as king for ever. (Ps 29:3–4, 10)

> Blessed are you Lord, God of all creation,
> In your wisdom and love you have given us the gift of water
> that comes down from the sky to refresh the earth,
> to nourish it, and make all things grow,
> to give seed for the sower and food to eat. (see Isaiah 55:10)
> Open our eyes to the wonders of your creation.

> Refresh and renew your people
> that we may serve each other in justice and with dignity
> for the glory of your name, Lord for ever and ever. Amen.

26. 'Praise of God creates community, advances harmony, and leads to the perfection of creation in history.' Erich Zenger in Erich Zenger and Frank-Lothar Hossfeld, *Psalms 3* (Hermeneia; Minneapolis: Fortress Press, 2011), 640.

2.2 The Soil Crisis: From Land Flowing with Milk and Honey to Wasteland[27]

> The only thing that stands between us and extinction is
> six inches of soil and the fact that it rains.
> (Anna Krzywoszynska, University of Sheffield)[28]

On Ash Wednesday, and sometimes at funerals, we hear the words: 'Dust you are, and unto dust you shall return' (Gen 3:19). The Bible, especially the Old Testament, brings out the intimate relationship between human beings and the earth. Biblical imagination is profoundly ecological. Humanity's first name, Adam, is a play on *adamah*, the Hebrew for 'earth' or 'ground': the Bible makes it very plain that we come from the earth (see also Gen 2:7). Moreover, when the time comes for us to die, we return to the earth – 'ashes to ashes and dust to dust' – where our bodily remains are laid to rest (see Ecclesiastes 12:7). Human beings are not above nature; spiritual and all as we are, we are fully part of nature.

Pope Francis expresses it thus, 'The earth was here before us and it has been given to us' (*Laudato Si'*, 67). This sentiment finds deep resonance within Irish culture, with its strong tradition of esteeming the beauty of the land and preserving it for future generations.

Within ecological circles, some controversy surrounds God's mandate to humanity: 'Be fruitful and multiply and fill the earth and subdue it; and have dominion over the fish of the sea and over the birds of the air and over every living thing that moves upon the earth' (Gen 1:28). Such an emphasis on human power has long been regarded as supporting a culture of environmental irresponsibility.[29] God-given 'dominion'

27. See *Laudato Si'*, 140.
28. See 'How Soil Offers Hope for the Climate Crisis', filmed July 2019 for *The Guardian*, UK, video, https://youtu.be/BSHR4sUZpcw. Accessed 9 July 2021. Dr Anna Krzywoszynska is a research fellow in the Faculty of Social Sciences at Sheffield, where she is also an associate director at the University of Sheffield Institute for Sustainable Food.

29. In a seminal article in 1967, American medievalist Lynn T. White Jr argued that religions – particularly Western Christianity – are major drivers of worldwide ecological crises, because of their conviction that a religious world view can justify human domination of the planet. He argued that such a world view could only be effectively countered from a religious perspective. See

does not, however, mean absolute domination. In the words of *Laudato Si'*, '[N]owadays we must forcefully reject the notion that our being created in God's image and given dominion over the earth justifies absolute domination over other creatures' (*Laudato Si'*, 67). When God shares his dominion with us, it is not so that we can destroy the planet, but so that we can do as God does; in other words, so that we can participate in caring for it (see Gen 2 and Ps 147:8–9).[30] At its heart, this is a call to human stewardship of creation. We have a God-given responsibility to care for the earth.

From the beginning of ancient civilisation, human beings have left their mark upon the earth. With the discovery of new continents and their apparently infinite natural resources, with the arrival of the Industrial Revolution, followed by advances in science and the rise of modern technology, many societies and economies began to view the earth as something simply to be exploited.[31] The culture of care was

---

'The Historical Roots of Our Ecologic Crisis', *Science* 155 (10 March 1967): 1203–77. In 1973, in a follow-up essay, White would further assert, 'What people do about their ecology depends on what they think about themselves in relation to things around them.' Until we 'think about fundamentals ... clarify our thinking ... rethink our axioms ... we will not adequately address our environmental crisis.' People, White pointed out, 'commit their lives to what they consider good' (see 'Continuing the Conversation' in Ian G. Barbour [ed.], *Western Man and Environmental Ethics* [Reading, Mass.: Addison-Wesley, 1973], 55–64). Addressing the climate crisis is not simply a technological challenge; it is an ethical and moral challenge. At its core, it is a spiritual challenge: a challenge for us to discover what we are about, and what is worth living for. Here again, one touches an enduring truth in Christian education; namely,

that knowledge without values runs the risk of undermining that which it claims to foster (see Archbishop D. Farrell, Address to the Fellows of Trinity College, Trinity, 26 April 2021).

30. He covers the heavens with clouds,
prepares rain for the earth,
makes grass grow on the hills.

He gives to the animals their food,
and to the young ravens when
they cry.   (Ps 147:8–9 [NRSV])

31. When creation is seen as the property of any individual or group of individuals, it risks being ransacked for the benefit of a few. Pope Francis cites Pope Benedict's exhortation 'to realize that creation is harmed "where we ourselves have the final word, where everything is simply our property and we use it for ourselves alone. The misuse of creation begins when we no longer recognize any higher instance than ourselves, when we see nothing else but ourselves"' (*LS*, 6).

firmly replaced by a culture of profit, a culture that took without attending to the consequences of what it was doing. In recent decades, as tropical rainforests have been cut down and animal species have become extinct, we have become aware of the need to limit the human exploitation of nature. The industrialisation of agriculture and the drive towards monoculture have wreaked havoc on the environment: soils are depleted – sometimes in whole regions the ground becomes less productive, even to the point of desertification – ecosystems are destroyed and species disappear.[32] Seen from space, we inhabit a tiny blue dot within the vast solar system, and this tiny, beautiful blue planet is very fragile indeed.[33]

Ecological awareness is now growing. In recent years we have seen numerous initiatives to address the negative effects of our unbalanced exploitation of the earth.[34] One example – though not without controversy – is the re-wetting of bogs in the Midlands and elsewhere. People have been amazed and encouraged by the rich biodiversity that has re-established itself in these bogs. In cities also, we see strong support for communal gardens and green spaces. Our lives, and the lives of all creatures, are enriched by these developments. The whole community is in the debt of those whose imagination, dedication and energy have developed and maintain these projects.

Again, the Psalms – saturated with a concern for the earth and everything that dwells upon it – call us to wonder and praise. Their poetry provides a language that opens our hearts, so that we may begin to pray in thanksgiving for this planet and concern for its renewal.

32. 'God has joined us so closely to the world around us that we can feel the desertification of the soil almost as a physical ailment, and the extinction of a species as a painful disfigurement' (*Evangelii Gaudium*, 215). With the exponential loss of habitats in recent years, ecosystems which are interlinked are destroyed. See further the section on biodiversity below.

33. A famous image of earth taken in 1972 by the crew of the Apollo 17 spacecraft ('The Blue Marble') shows graphically the fragility of planet earth within the vast solar system.

34. Over-production of arable land will have devastating consequences when viewed over a long period of time. Sharing the planet means restricting our use of the land. We live in a finite planet with finite possibilities of growth. If the planet suffocates, our economies will also suffocate.

The Lord's is the earth and its fullness,
the world and all its inhabitants;
for upon the seas did He set it;
upon the rivers He made it firm.   (Ps 24:1–2)

All ... look to you
to give them their food in due season.
You send forth your spirit, they are created;
and you renew the face of the earth.   (Ps 104:27, 30)

Blessed are you, Lord God of all creation,
in your wisdom and love you have given your people the
gift of the soil.
In your goodness you made the earth bring forth vegetation:
plants yielding seed of every kind,
and trees of every kind bearing fruit.   (Gen 1:11)

Open our ears to the cry of the earth,
and our hearts to its call,
that we may cherish what you have given us,
care for it,
and share its fruits for the good of all.

2.3 The Biodiversity Crisis: The Breakdown of Biodiversity[35]

Our planet is home to a seemingly infinite variety of
species, from ocean giants to the tiniest insects ... But
today it's vanishing, at rates never seen before in human
history.   (David Attenborough)[36]

When we say 'biodiversity', we mean the abundance of life on
our planet. Sometimes because of the work, commitment and
conviction of broadcasters like David Attenborough and the
late Éamon de Buitléar (1930–2013), and sometimes because we
ourselves manage to 'take in' the wonder and complexity of the
natural environment, we are struck by the variety, beauty and
majesty of the natural world. The world God created overflows

---

35. See further *Laudato Si'*, 32–42.
36. David Attenborough in the opening
lines of his documentary, 'Extinction:
The Facts', BBC, September 2020,
rebroadcast on RTÉ One on 11 July
2021.

with life, and with its variety. From the opening lines of the Book of Genesis, with its 'in the beginning, God created ...' (Gen 1:1), to the closing lines of the Book of Revelation with its vision of the healing river of life (see Rev 22:1–5), the Scriptures bear witness to the richness, diversity and complexity of life on this planet and beyond. In spite of the 'many painful and chaotic experiences' they recount, the many voices of the Bible 'manage to say their fundamental "yes" to the world and to life in the world. In the midst of privation and anxiety, doubt and desperation, the people of the Bible seek to recognize, share in forming, and celebrate the earth as the location of the saving rule of God, and as the realm wherein life is given to them, as cosmos within chaos.'[37] Today in ways we never foresaw, and at a rate we cannot imagine, the God-given abundance and variety of life is disappearing before our eyes. Today we are living during the sixth largest extinction event since life began in the oceans 3.8 billion years ago. The last time something similar happened was 65 million years ago when the dinosaurs and many other species became extinct. A recent United Nations panel of experts has found that 1 million – one in four – animal and plant species face extinction within coming decades.[38] That's one eighth of the total biodiversity of our planet. This is about much more than losing strange or interesting animals. At stake is the earth's ability to provide us and other creatures with clean air, fresh water, good quality soil and pollination for our crops, even future life-saving medicines. Recent research has shown that in parts of continental Europe, 41 per cent of insect species have declined in the past forty years. They have declined in Ireland also. The shocking reality is that extinction is forever.[39] The Bible, particularly the prophetic books, is no

37. Karl Löning and Erich Zenger, *To Begin with, God Created: Biblical Theologies of Creation* (Collegeville: Liturgical Press, 2000), 188–9. This volume arose from a paper at a conference organised by Löning and Zenger (d. 2010) in 1996, the papers of which were published in German in 1997. The intervening twenty-five years have done nothing to lessen the concerns expressed.

38. United Nations report from the Intergovernmental Science-Policy Platform on Biodiversity and Ecosystem Services, 6 May 2019.

39. In *Laudato Si'*, Patriarch Bartholomew is clear that 'to destroy the biological diversity of God's creation' is sinful (*LS*, 8). Pope Francis also uses quite strong language in relation to this issue, noting, 'The earth is beginning to look more and more like an immense pile of filth' (*LS*, 21).

stranger to the threat to the land and to the devastation that follows in the wake of war, conquest and oppression.

> For even though the fig does not blossom,
> nor fruit grow on the vine,
> even though the olive crop fails,
> and fields produce no harvest,
> even though flocks vanish from the folds
> and stalls stand empty of cattle ...   (Hab 3:17)

When we read the Scriptures sensitively, the Word of God bears constant witness to the interrelatedness of the processes of our world, as we can hear in Amos's answer to Amaziah, 'I am no prophet ... but I am a herdsman, and a dresser of sycamore trees' (Amos 7:14). The various aspects of his life are intertwined: his shepherding, his care of nature, his call to be God's prophet.

The various aspects of our lives are also intertwined: our cities and towns, our farms, our gardens are brimming with life in all its variety and diversity. As the biodiversity crisis brings home to us, all life on this planet is interconnected. Living responsibly demands of us patterns of consumption that nurture and foster the diversity of life on this planet, and permits people to prosper in a sustainable way. This calls for fundamental changes in our patterns of consumption (for example, a greater attention to the use of local and seasonal food), in our approach to waste, and a corresponding change of mindset and priorities. In the end, this will mean profound societal and economic change. Clearly, while every person and every household has responsibility and a role to play, local and national governments, as well as international agencies, have a pivotal contribution to make. Again, this needs a both-and approach: *both* individual *and* societal.

For people of faith, let us give praise and thanks to God who created this wonderful world. We join with the praise and prayer of the psalmist:

> How many are your works, O Lord!
> In wisdom you have made them all.
> The earth is full of your creatures. ...

All of these look to you
to give them their food in due season.
You give it, they gather it up:
you open your hand, they have their fill.   (Ps 104:24, 27–8)

Blessed are you, Lord God of all creation,
in your love you have created all earth's creatures,
and in your wisdom you chose to share your life with all.
Send forth your Spirit   (Ps 104:30)
open the eyes of your people,
give sight to the blind   (Ps 146:8)
so that all your creatures may see your face,   (Ps 104:29)
and the whole universe rejoice in your works.   (Ps 104:31)

2.4 The Migration Crisis: Climate Change and Increasing Injustice[40]

People rarely drop dead on the street, but die quietly in
their poorly insulated and un-air-conditioned homes.
                    (Friederike Otto, University of Oxford)[41]

The message coming from the scientists is clear and unequivocal.
It requires a fundamental rethink on the part of the Church as
to how we think about and act on the climate and biodiversity
emergency. However, if we see things only in terms of climate
and technology, we miss the true dimensions of this tragedy
which is unfolding around us. As stated above, Pope Saint John
Paul II and Patriarch Bartholomew saw clearly that the challenge
the world faces 'is not simply economic and technological; it is
moral and spiritual'. They concluded that any enduring solution
requires, 'an inner change of heart. [Only this] can lead to a
change in lifestyle and of unsustainable patterns of consumption

---

40. See further *Laudato Si'*, 43–52.
41. See 'How Heatwaves became Climate Change's Silent Killer', *Financial Times*, 3 July 2021, 9. Dr Friederike Otto is associate director of the Environmental Change Institute at the University of Oxford, and a world-renowned expert on extreme weather events. Her research seeks to understand whether, and to what extent, extreme weather events are made more likely or intense due to climate change, as well as the impacts of man-made climate change on natural and social systems with a particular focus on Africa and India.

and production.'[42] To be clear, at the heart of the climate crisis lies a human crisis: the world which sees itself as lord and master of the earth, and feels entitled to plunder it at will (see *LS*, 2), *also sees itself as lord and master of others, and feels entitled to take them for granted and to take from them at will.* Plundering the earth and plundering the poor go hand in hand. It is, therefore, no surprise that the cry of the earth and the cry of the poor arise together. 'We need to strengthen the conviction that we are one single human family. There are no frontiers or barriers, political or social, behind which we can hide, still less is there room for the globalization of indifference' (*LS*, 52). We may not walk by on the other side (see Luke 10:31–2). We must get involved with the plundered earth and its wounded peoples.[43] Pope Francis has reflected on this complex issue, which lies at the very heart of the climate crisis. There will be no solution to this crisis without facing up to our obligations to our sisters and brothers whom the West has left behind.[44] The 'inseparable bond between concern for nature, justice for the poor, commitment to society, and interior peace' (*LS*, 10) is the true foundation of the way out of this crisis, which is in fact the way to life.

42. Pope Saint John Paul II and Patriarch Bartholomew I, 'Common Declaration on Environmental Ethics', 10 June 2002, www.vatican.va/content/john-paul-ii/en/speeches/2002/june/documents/hf_jp-ii_spe_20020610_venice-declaration.html.

43. American theologian Mary Frohlich, in exploring 'the depth of the spiritual transformation that is needed to address the reality of' climate change, keenly observed that the path for anyone who commits to engaging with the climate catastrophe mirrors the path of those who would commit themselves to the poor. Drawing on the work of Dominican theologian Albert Nolan, she outlines the four stages of a spiritual transformation that such a 'conversion' requires: (i) compassion – touching the earth, risking first-hand exposure to the crisis; (ii) structural change – nothing will truly change unless the economic and governmental structures that maintain the status quo change; (iii) humility – only a thoroughgoing divestment of egotism can enable one to endure the time of profound loss and abandonment that the commitment to change demands; (iv) solidarity – one must wholeheartedly experience oneself in communion with all affected, working and struggling with them rather than for them. See Mary Frohlich RSCJ, 'Under the Sign of Jonah: Studying Spirituality in a Time of Ecosystemic Crisis', *Spiritus: A Journal of Christian Spirituality* 9 (2009): 27–45. Reprinted in Charles E. Curran and Lisa A Fullam, *Ethics and Spirituality: Readings in Moral Theology* No. 17 (New York: Paulist, 2014), 206–28.

44. See Pope Saint Paul VI in his message for World Day of Peace 1972: 'If you want peace, work for justice.'

The psalmist, for whom justice and creation are inseparable, proposes this essential unity as the foundation of God's kingdom and our prayer.

> The Lord is king, let earth rejoice,
> let all the coastlands be glad.
> Cloud and darkness are God's raiment;
> justice and right, the foundation of God's throne.
>
> (Psalm 97:1–2)

3. The Climate Crisis: A Multi-layered Crisis

The climate crisis is not simply a crisis of our climate. No, it is a crisis with many dimensions, many layers. Environmental and social issues are interrelated, and because of that 'a true ecological approach always becomes a social approach' (*LS*, 49). It is a crisis that reflects how we treat each other and how we treat our world, that has deep roots in our choices. It is a crisis that has religious and inter-religious dimensions. It is a crisis that reflects a crisis in the human heart; in a real sense it is a spiritual crisis. Like every true crisis, it has the capacity to destroy us, but it also has the capacity to bring us to a new way of life.[45]

3.1 The Climate Crisis and Our Choices

While the climate crisis is played out in the natural world, its causes lie in human choices, in the choices of our economies and of our governments, and in our choices.[46] This means that the climate crisis is a profoundly human crisis with deep ethical, spiritual and religious dimensions. It will only be solved if we change: we need an 'inner change of heart ... a change in lifestyle', to return to the insight of Pope Saint John Paul II and Patriarch Bartholomew.[47] This means at the moral level a greater emphasis

---

45. See Pope Francis, Letter to Cardinal Reinhard Marx, 10 June 2021.

46. In *Laudato Si'*, 208, Pope Francis says it is morally imperative that we take responsibility for what we are doing. We are to act now to slow down the trends and make every effort to prevent further damage. This requires a change of heart and lifestyles and establishing new ways of producing, distributing and consuming.

47. When Jesus teaches his disciples about living their faith through prayer, care for the poor, and fasting, he asks his hearers to look at things in a new way: when they pray, they are to go to a hidden place, and their Father who sees what is hidden will reward them (see Matt 6:5–8). Similarly, when they give to those in need, they are not to let their left hand know what their right hand is doing, so that their alms may

on justice: social, intergenerational, and climate justice. We do well to ask: is it just that those who contribute least to the climate crisis suffer the most from its effects, especially the poor but also the younger generations?

In *Laudato Si'* Pope Francis asks a very important question: 'What kind of world do we want to leave to those who come after us, to children who are now growing up?' (*LS*, 160) This is the same question being asked of us right now by the young people of the world. In May 2019, Pope Francis met the young Swedish climate activist Greta Thunberg. He congratulated her on her work and urged her to continue. Greta is a shining example of the power of one person to effect change. In the gospel Jesus says, 'I have come that you may have life and live it to the full' (John 10:10). But our life is also our life together. What does this fullness of life together look like for future generations in a world of ecological breakdown? Is this what we want to give to our children?

This calls us to *solidarity*. We have seen during the Covid-19 crisis the difference solidarity makes in effecting change. Something similar is required in addressing the climate crisis. We are in this together. This is our crisis. It is vital that we act together. There is no other way.

Solidarity, therefore, calls us to compassion. Without feeling the need of our sisters and brothers, and the needs of everything that God has created, we will be unable to address the climate emergency. If we take seriously the first sentence of the Creed – 'We believe in *one* God ...' – we proclaim that the *one* God in whom we believe is the *one* Creator of heaven and earth, and of *all* creation. There is not one Creator for humanity, and another for other forms of life. The climate crisis 'makes clear that the human species and the natural world will flourish or collapse together'.[48] Rather than subduing the earth, must we hear anew

---

be given in hiddenness; and the Father who sees what is hidden will reward them (Matt 6:3–4). So too with fasting (see Matt 6:16–18). The thrust is clear: the heart of prayer is in our hearts. That is not to say that public worship is not important, but the public worship of a people 'whose heart is far from God' (see Matt 15:8, where Jesus cites Isaiah 29:1) is but a shell of worship and prayer. Prayer, justice, and authentic expressions of faith flow from the heart, and return to our hearts bringing new nourishment and new life.

48. See Elizabeth A. Johnson, *Ask the Beasts* (New York and London: Bloomsbury, 2014), 3.

God's call to Adam – and therefore to us all – to 'till the earth and keep it' (Gen 2:15)?

Compassion is our capacity to feel and be moved by the pain and trouble of others. We remember the Good Samaritan: what sets him apart is his compassion for the wounded man abandoned on the road (see Luke 10:33). We are called to hear not only the cry of the poor, but also the cry of the earth (see *LS*, 49). This means that the climate crisis is a profoundly human and, therefore, a profoundly spiritual crisis.

3.2 The Climate Crisis as a Spiritual Crisis

The climate crisis is a deeply spiritual crisis, posing searching questions about human identity. The human is more than a material being and more than a biological entity that will dissolve in time. Every human being, created by God, is endowed with dignity and freedom, conscience and consciousness. More and more, people are valuing the importance of consciousness, especially reflective self-consciousness that opens up the human spirit to the possibility of an interior life and a religious commitment.

Much of our culture has lost a sense of interconnectedness with one another and with God's creation. Our faith offers us a wonderful vision to rekindle these relationships, to renew a childlike sense of awe, wonder and beauty, and thus set out in living the first commandment God gave to us, to be guardians and protectors of this beautiful world, not its polluters and destroyers. We are called to look out at the world and see that, 'soil, water, mountains: everything is, as it were, a caress of God' (*LS*, 84). God in his goodness embraces us in the world into which he has created us: its light, its darkness, its mystery, its paradoxes and its promise. Thus, the psalmist prays:

> When I see the heavens, the work of your hands,
> the moon and the stars which you arranged,
> what are we that you should keep us in mind,
> mere mortals that you care for us?   (Ps 8:4–5)

3.3 The Climate Crisis as a Religious Challenge

The climate challenge is, therefore, ultimately a religious challenge. A religious view of the world – and this is the case for *all* the major religions of the world – offers a vision, promotes

values, encourages harmony with nature, and connects people with the beauty and wonder of creation. Faith communities the world over have a contribution to make to the current debate about climate crisis, the pollution of our oceans, the depletion of soil, the loss of biodiversity, and the cost of all this to all God's creatures. In confronting this crisis for our planet, all the world's religions have a vital contribution to make. We remember the words of Jesus: 'Whoever is not against us is for us' (Mark 9:40). 'It must ... be kept in mind that every quest of the human spirit for truth and goodness ... is inspired by the Holy Spirit.'[49] Recognising 'the seeds of the Word' present and active in the various religions (*Ad Gentes*, 11; *Lumen Gentium*, 17), in our land and across the world, let us seek opportunities where people of all faiths and none can together nurture the fruitfulness of land and sea, making it truly what God created it to be: our common home, a place of blessing. In the Holy Spirit, who is present in humanity's religious quest,[50] who 'blows where it wills' (see John 3:8),[51] and whose power renews the face of the earth, we pray:

> Let the peoples praise you, O God;
> let all the peoples praise you.
> The earth has yielded its fruit
> for God, our God, has blessed us.
> May God still give us his blessing
> till the ends of the earth revere him.   (Ps 67:6–8)

3.4 The Climate Crisis as an Absence of Solidarity

'It is not good that Adam should be alone' (Gen 2:18). God's global address from the opening pages of the Bible is a privileged window on how human beings truly are. We are created to be with others. God put into our bodies and into our hearts the desire, and indeed the need, to be with others. What Saint Augustine so eloquently said of our hearts – that they shall not rest until they rest in God[52] – applies equally to our God-given call to be with each other, and *for* each other. The lawyer's question

---

49. Pope Saint John Paul II, General Audience, 9 September 1998.

50. Pope Saint John Paul II, General Audience, 9 September 1998.

51. See also Pope Saint John Paul II, *Redemptor Hominis*, 6, 12.

52. *Cor nostrum inquietum est donec requiescat in te*. Augustine, *Confessions*, 1.1.

to Jesus, 'Who is my neighbour?' (Luke 10:29) is not some once-off remark in a chance encounter. Rather, it is a question that addresses the core of what it means to be human.

This is not to discount the need for solitude and silence. Silence and solitude are best seen as an encounter with ourselves, and not a flight from the world or from its challenges and its oftentimes-painful realities. Christian faith, far from being a flight from the demands of living well with our neighbour, challenges us to meet our neighbour well: to risk seeing the other, reaching out to the other, listening to what the other expresses – spoken and unspoken – to seeing what the other needs. Our tradition calls this solidarity. It means living in the world as it is. It means moving beyond our self-made worlds and entering the world God gives us.[53]

> Solidarity means much more than engaging in sporadic acts of generosity. It means thinking and acting in terms of community. It means that the lives of all are prior to the appropriation of goods by a few. It also means combatting the structural causes of poverty, inequality, the lack of work, land and housing, the denial of social and labour rights. It means confronting the destructive effects of the empire of money. *(Fratelli Tutti*, 116)[54]

53. Pope Saint John Paul II put it this way: 'When interdependence becomes recognized ... the correlative response as a moral and social attitude, as a "virtue" is solidarity. This then is not a feeling of vague compassion or shallow distress at the misfortunes of so many people, both near and far. On the contrary, it is a firm and persevering determination to commit oneself to the common good; that is to say to the good of all and of each individual, because we are all really responsible for all' (*Sollicitudo Rei Socialis*, 38). Solidarity is also about more than action: our solidarity with each other, especially with the poor and with those on the many margins of our world, is also an in-breaking of God's kingdom into the world. When, in true solidarity, our hearts become one with our neighbour, light shines into the darkness (see John 1:5): there is a breach in the fortresses of injustice, exclusion, and degradation. And light shines also into our own hearts: we recognise our own darkness, our solidarity with the indifference, disengagement and harshness of the world. The deep movement of God's mercy calls us home.

54. Solidarity has been a fundamental concern in Pope Francis's ministry. Solidarity, and the service that flows from it, are never ideological. We serve people, not an idea. Justice blossoms where love is open to all. See *Fratelli Tutti*, 115.

Solidarity, in its deepest meaning, is a way of living in the world. It is why God sent his son into the world: to be one with us, to be in solidarity with all that we are, and with all that he created. If God chose the way of solidarity as the way of salvation, do we have a choice in living in solidarity with each other? In the end, solidarity is expressed in involved committed care. And involved committed care is ultimately expressed not only in words but also in deeds; care is expressed in service. 'Solidarity finds concrete expression in service' (*Fratelli Tutti*, 115). Service of people, if it is to be more than immediate and episodic, must address the structural issues that keep sections of society, or whole regions of the world, in situations of enduring disadvantage. Today, the devastating effects of climate change mean that service of our vulnerable and marginalised sisters and brothers can no longer be fragmented, failing to address the root causes and drivers of injustice. True service must address climate change, both globally and locally. To apply to the call to justice the admonition of Jesus, 'Not everyone who says to me "Lord, Lord," will enter the kingdom of heaven' (Matt 7:21), one might say, 'Not everyone who says, "Justice, justice," is serving justice well, but those who do what justice demands.' In our world transformed by the climate crisis, justice requires care for creation, environmental engagement, the protection of ecosystems – and all who dwell in them. In other words, integral and holistic care of the poor and of all life (see *LS*, 137–62). This means change: change of horizon, change of priorities, change of expectations, change of lifestyle. It amounts to nothing less than a conversion, one that might be termed an 'ecological conversion'.[55] It is to this we must now turn.

4. Responding to the Climate Crisis

What Pope Francis has said about the 'catastrophe ... of sexual abuse and the way the Church has dealt with it until

55. Again, one needs to avoid a false contrast between moral conversion and 'ecological conversion'. In the current crisis, the moral response to Christ's call has an essential ecological dimension. Morality in the Judeo-Christian tradition, particularly in its Catholic expression, has never been a 'private' morality; it always has a social dimension. We see this in Catholic social teaching, in the Church's concern for the family (even if at times we have been misguided in the 'application' of this teaching), and in its concern for the dignity of work. The call to environmental responsibility flows seamlessly from this tradition.

recently'[56] also applies to the looming climate catastrophe: first, that not everyone can accept the reality of the crisis; second, that action is needed; third, that involvement is required; and fourth, that 'ostrich' politics – the politics of denial and paralysis – are not an option.

It is important that we permit the Holy Father to speak with his own voice. He says:

> Not everyone wants to accept this reality [of climate crisis], but it is the only way, because making 'resolutions' to change one's life without 'having skin in the game' leads to nothing.[57] Personal, social, and historical realities are concrete, and are not to be engaged with ideas; because ideas are discussed – and it is good that they are – but reality must always be engaged and discerned. ... In my opinion, every Bishop of the Church must take this on board and ask himself, 'What must I do in the face of this catastrophe?'

We are called to act, to move beyond a half-hearted acknowledgment of a crisis, which is in reality a hidden denial. We cannot continue to keep our head in the sand when the world around us is being turned into a desert. To let Pope Francis speak again:

> Ostrich politics lead nowhere; this crisis has to be engaged by our Easter faith. ... Taking the crisis on board – personally and communally – is the only fruitful path, because one does not come through a crisis alone: one comes though [a crisis] in community; and one must also remember that one exits a crisis a better or worse person, but [a crisis] never leaves the person unchanged.

56. The phrase is taken from Pope Francis's letter to Cardinal Reinhard Marx, 10 June 2021. The letter – Pope Francis's response to Cardinal Marx's letter of resignation – is an important statement on how bishops in particular, and the Church in general, might respond to the deep crisis occasioned by the sexual abuse of minors.

57. Pope Francis used the South American idiom, without 'putting the meat on the grill' (*sin 'poner la carne sobre el asador'*), which means without being invested in that about which we talk and debate.

Faith is the opposite to resignation. People of faith are people who act, since 'authentic faith ... always involves a deep desire to change the world, to transmit values, to leave this earth somehow better than we found it' (*EG*, 183). That is not to avoid addressing limit and failure. Christ himself had to do so on the cross. But it would be a betrayal of the cross and of its power to make of it a veil to cover our own inaction and our own lack of conviction.

Action in the face of the climate crisis demands a change of priorities. In a real sense, it requires a conversion. To borrow a phrase from the world of architecture and design, our culture – and therefore our lifestyles – must learn that less can be more. If our cup is too full, how can we receive? Here is the mystery of Christ: it is in giving that we receive, it is in dying to ourselves that we are born to the life that endures. Anyone who has ever loved has discovered this.

This conversion enables us to see the world with gratitude as God's loving gift (*LS*, 220), to realise that everything in the world is interrelated and interconnected, and that within the chaos and suffering of our world there is an underlying order and dynamism that we have no right to ignore (*LS*, 221).

It is our encounter with Christ in creation, in the gospels, in each other, and in the life of the Church that effects ecological conversion. For others it will be the discovery of the indwelling presence of the Spirit in the rhythms of the natural world, in the beauty of creation and in each other that brings about conversion.[58]

4.1 The Call to Ecological Conversion

In light of all that has been said above, it is clear that care for creation 'is not an optional or a secondary aspect of our Christian experience' (*LS*, 217), but rather defines who we are as a Christian people.[59] '[T]he ecological crisis is also a summons to profound

58. Alongside the gift of the Spirit of God in the world there is also the presence of Christ as the Word of God: 'In the beginning was the Word ... and the Word was with God ... and the Word became flesh and lived among us' in Jesus of Nazareth (John 1:1–15). Through the Incarnation 'God has united himself definitively to the earth' (*LS*, 245). For Christians, Christ is at the centre of creation: 'the first born of all creation' (Col 1:15). Further, 'Christ has taken unto himself this material world and now risen, is intimately present to each being surrounding it with his affection' (LS, 221, 100).

59. God has always guided the Church, the People of God, in a way that progressively 'reveals Himself and makes known to us the hidden purpose of His will' (Vatican II, *Dei Verbum*, 2, citing Eph 1:9). In the early

interior conversion ... Living our vocation to be protectors of God's handiwork is essential to a life of virtue' (*LS*, 217). This crisis demands of us a conversion, one that can be termed an ecological conversion.

At the dawn of time, God's creating Spirit was poured out on creation: as it says in the psalm, 'By the word of the Lord the heavens were made, by the breath of his mouth all the stars' (Psalm 33:6). God's Spirit still fills the universe, and makes all of creation a place that is holy, a sacred place: 'The Spirit ... is intimately present at the very heart of the universe' (*LS*, 238), 'the life of the Spirit is not dissociated from the body or from nature or from worldly realities, but lived in and with them, in communion with all that surrounds us.' This is why Pope Francis encourages us to adopt an 'ecological spirituality', a spirituality that 'can motivate us to a more passionate concern for the protection of our world' (*LS*, 216). At the centre of this spirituality is a rediscovery of the gift of the Spirit and of the sacredness of God's creation. It amounts to a call to living in another way. It is a true call to conversion.

5. Ecological Conversion: Towards a Culture of Care
Recent years have witnessed the publication of many important reports on the environment; however, life teaches us that reports alone will not mitigate the climate crisis, its effects, or bring about the realisation of the targets from agreements such as the Paris Climate Agreement of 2015. Important as they are, ideas

---

centuries, the Church under the guidance of the Holy Spirit, learned the depth of the mystery of Jesus, God's only son. In a later age, we were brought to understand the contours of the community of faith that is the Church. In the last century, the Church turned anew towards our obligation to the neighbour, and we have seen a flourishing in Catholic social teaching. In our own time, in this crisis, we are being asked to turn toward creation, and to rediscover what we had lost sight of: how God creates us, where He places us, and what He now asks of us for the survival of our planet, and for our own salvation. Like all growth, this long journey has not been straightforward, but has been filled with controversy and the misunderstanding that comes from differing visions of who we are and who God is. Yet, this is how God reveals his truth to his people on their pilgrim way. It is important that we keep this before us, as we reflect on the climate crisis. In the cry of the earth, it is God himself who calls us. A living faith will seek to discover the will of the living God who is revealing himself in this crisis.

and discussion will not change the concrete situation. The agreed targets are hard to meet, and many countries are struggling to meet the pledges they made under the Paris Agreement to reduce their greenhouse gas emissions. While several EU countries have achieved significant reductions, other countries, including our own, face difficult decisions. As a country, we need to ask how we can meet the solemn undertakings we gave to the developed world, to countries that invest in ours, and by implication to hard-pressed countries in the rest of the world, as far back as 2008. This calls for courage, honesty, humility and imagination to accept our role in addressing the injustices that continue to keep our sisters and brothers in the poorer parts of the world in situations of disadvantage, rob them of true hope, and force many to consider leaving their homeland. Here we perceive the deeper roots of the migration crisis that touches many regions of the world. It is not only because of war that people flee their land. The flight to more prosperous regions is also due to the lack of hope in being able to have a life that offers an acceptable level of freedom, well-being and dignity in their own country. The 'tragic rise in the number of migrants seeking to flee from growing poverty' is profoundly linked to 'environmental degradation. They are not recognized by international conventions as refugees; they bear the loss of the lives they have left behind, without enjoying any legal protection whatsoever. Sadly, there is widespread indifference to [and sometimes cynicism in the face of] such suffering' (*LS*, 25).

The developed world, which includes Ireland, needs to approach things in a different way. We need a new vision for living and sharing the fruits of our common home. This demands viable alternatives to the patterns of economic life and the cycles of growth that benefit the few at the cost of the many. 'We need to reject a magical conception of the market, which would suggest that problems can be solved simply by an increase in the profits of companies or individuals ... Where profits alone count, there can be ... no serious thought for the real value of things, their significance for persons and cultures, or the concerns and needs of the poor' (*LS*, 190). Such behavioural change is only sustainable when rooted in values that make sense to people, and make sense of our lives. Bringing about change within the climate emergency is a slow process and requires not only short-term initiatives but also long-term planning and vision. We owe this to our children, to the generations coming after us.

When we read and hear the gospels, we see Christ putting before his hearers a vision of the world that was in sharp contrast to the operative vision of many of his contemporaries: turning the other cheek (Matt 5:39) rather than hitting back was his way of overcoming violence; going the second mile (Matt 5:41) rather than resisting was his way of overcoming the oppressor; being reconciled with your opponent (Matt 5:23–6) rather than conquering them was his way to enduring peace. Patience, kindness, humility, welcome, openness became the marks of the rule of God, and the signs of God's presence among the people of God and in the world (see 1 Cor 13:4–7, Luke 24:29). Christ presents us with another horizon. In Christ, God calls us to live in another way. In our decisions – large and small – we are presented with a choice: do we follow Christ in his way – a way of welcome and gentleness, compassion and mercy – or do we choose exclusion and harshness, rough justice and a distance which is the mark of hardness of heart. Those who follow Jesus are asked credibly to present to the world another way of being in the world, another way of living together in harmony and dignity with all who share this planet – our only home. As the young never cease to remind us, 'There is no Planet B.'

At a societal level, a developed economy and society like Ireland cannot let itself off the hook. It cannot 'pass by on the other side' (Luke 10:30–1). This means embracing a culture of care for our common home and *all who dwell in it* (see Psalm 24:1). Developing a culture of care – the foundation of which is already laid in our faith – is essential if the world is to 'combat the culture of indifference, waste and confrontation' that imperils our planet and our very selves.[60] While there are many characteristics of a *culture of care*, I wish to underline four:

- A sense of GRATITUDE and WONDER for the gift that we have received in this beautiful place, and in this extraordinary planet.
- A SENSITIVITY towards and a commitment to the vulnerable, the weak, the defenceless, the voiceless, and

60. See Pope Francis, Message for the Celebration of the 54th World Day of Peace, Rome, 8 December 2020, 1.

those who are invisible and disadvantaged in our society and in our world.

- An ACTIVE INVESTMENT in people and in the environment, since we invest time and resources in what is important to us. The Samaritan *invests* in the man he finds on the road. In this stranger, he invests his time and his money (see Luke 10:35).
- A sense of FINITUDE and LIMIT: everything is finite – the oceans, the soil, the air we breathe, the lives of people. Appreciating the finite character of all that God created transforms how we engage with it.

Two of these four characteristics merit further comment. To embody a *culture of care* means putting flesh on the values we espouse. Our daily lives give expression to the values we live. This is what we mean by our spirituality. Developing a spirituality of gratitude and wonder, of finitude and limit, permits us to become agents of change in this important time.

5.1 Developing a Spirituality of Gratitude and Wonder

A sense of GRATITUDE and WONDER for the gift that we have received in this beautiful place, and in this extraordinary planet.

When we come to our senses, we realise that we did not 'make' this planet, and much less did we make the universe. Anyone who has had the opportunity to contemplate the night sky, and look in wonder at the Milky Way, arrives at a sense of things that is in contrast to planning and construction. Opening one's eyes to the magnitude and majesty of it all provokes both bafflement and awe. Given any bit of quiet and any stretch of time, we are confronted with the mystery of it all. It is no different when we contemplate the complexity and fragility of a flower, or look closely at a leaf, or a swarm of bees or birds. The universe outside is mirrored in the universe within. The words of the psalm come to mind:

When I see the heavens, the work of your hands,
the moon and the stars which you arranged,
what are mortals that you should keep us in mind,
mere creatures that you care for us?   (Ps 8:3–5)

In the end, the universe, and all within it, is a gift. To marvel and give thanks is the most appropriate response. To give thanks is also a healthy response. Gratitude, so vital to our own well-being, is also vital for the survival of our planet.

When we're grateful towards something or someone, our fundamental stance changes. We no longer take that person, or that reality for granted. They are no longer there for the taking; they are no longer there to be plundered. This holds for people; and this holds for our common home.

Gratitude is the spontaneous response of a healthy mind and body to life. But gratitude is much more than saying thanks. Gratitude is an embrace of life. Every day, every person has to make a practical choice between embracing life or keeping life at a distance, between trusting life or not trusting life. Keeping life at a distance, distrusting life, ultimately leads to misery, a living death. On the other hand, trusting life and whatever comes up leads to life. It opens the door to seeing every moment, every person and every place as a gift. With the psalmist one can pray:

> I thank you, Lord, with all my heart,
> you have heard the words of my mouth.
> I thank you for your faithfulness and love
> which excel all we ever knew of you.
> On the day I called, you answered;
> you increased the strength of my soul.
> You stretch out your hand and save me,
> your hand will do all things for me.
> Your love, O Lord, is eternal,
> discard not the work of your hands.　　(Ps 138:1–3, 7b–8)

For the person of faith, to give thanks *for* the gift is to give thanks *to* the Giver, and it is more: it is to say to our Heavenly Father, 'We belong with you.' Giver and thanks-giver belong together. Eternal life has already begun (see John 17:3); heaven and earth are touching.[61] We are standing on holy ground.

61. See 'Monks in Our Midst: David Steind-Rast on Gratitude', Monastries of the Heart, accessed 5 July 2021, www.monasteriesoftheheart.org/monks-our-midst/david-steindl-rast-gratitude-1. Brother David Steindl-Rast is a Benedictine monk of the community of Mount Savior Monastery in Elmira, NY, and an important teacher of gratitude as a spiritual way.

5.2 Developing a Spirituality of Finitude and Limit

> A sense of FINITUDE AND LIMIT. Everything is finite: the
> oceans, the soil, the air we breathe, the lives of people.
> Appreciating the finite character of all that God created
> transforms how we engage with it.

In our finite world, there can no longer be a place for a throwaway
culture, or an economy that is built on obsolescence. The reality
that the lifespan of each person, and of each creature, is limited
might alert us to something fundamental in the character
of created life. From the perspective of faith, the gospels'
unwavering insistence on the reality of Jesus' death drives home
the same existential truth. Our capacity to come to terms with
finitude and limit – be it of our own existence or of the resources
we have available to us – is essential to our becoming fully alive
and fully human. Former Archbishop of Canterbury Rowan
Williams names well what is at stake:

> the fantasy that we can as individuals halt the passage of
> time and change, and the illusions we cherish that the
> human race can somehow behave as though it were not in
> fact embedded in the material world ... Personal neurosis
> and *collective ecological disaster* are the manifest effects
> of this sort of denial. And the more sophisticated we
> become in handling our environment and creating
> virtual worlds to inhabit and control, the looser our grip
> becomes on the inexorable continuity between our own
> organic existence and the rest of the world we live in.[62]

This applies to soil, and air, and sea. Even the vast ocean of this
blue planet cannot for much longer absorb the waste – organic,
urban and industrial – that has been recklessly and cynically
dumped into it for decades.[63]

---

62. Rowan Williams, 'How dying offers us a chance to live the fullest life', *New Statesman* (15 April 2018), https://www.newstatesman.com/culture/books/2018/04/how-dying-offers-us-chance-live-fullest-life. Emphasis added.

63. With the 8 million tons of plastic that end up in the oceans each year, it is to be feared that the prediction that there will be more plastic than fish in the sea by 2050 is more than an alarmist's tale. A special report in the journal *Science*

To embrace this is to strive to establish a deep unity in our lives. It means overcoming the fragmentation of existence that erodes all that permits us truly to be at home in the life for which God has created us. We begin to realise that addressing the climate crisis is not simply an ecological challenge, but is an existential challenge. In the climate crisis, God asks us not only what type of environment we want to inhabit, but also what type of life do we wish to embrace. In 'God's Grandeur', his hope-filled poem, Gerard Manley Hopkins draws his hearers' attention to 'the dearest freshness' that lives 'deep down things'. This is the life, the deep and wonderful life, God wills for all his creatures.

6. Sustaining a Culture of Care: Prayer and Community

Prayer and community are the two great sustainers of the Christian life.

6.1 Creation and Prayer

6.1.1 The Prayer of the Christian

> That place where God dwells in me is also the place of prayer. Long before I am aware of it or before I take interest in it, this prayer is going on ceaselessly within me.
> (André Louf OCSO)[64]

in late June 2021 launched a campaign for governments to commit to phase out 'virgin' plastic production in the next twenty years. Even if that happens, the detritus of our age will remain a feature of the oceans for centuries to come. In *Let Us Dream*, Pope Francis tells of the fishermen from the Italian town of San Benedetto del Tronto who told him of the tons of plastic they had fished up from the sea. He continues, 'Theirs is a fleet of small boats, crews of no more than maybe six or seven on board each one. This year they came to see me again and told me they had hauled up twenty-four tons of garbage of which about half – that's twelve tons – was plastic. They've taken it upon themselves as a kind of mission not to throw it back in the water. So along with the fish, they

gather the plastic and separate it on the boats – which costs money, of course.' The Holy Father concludes, '*Laudato Si'* links the scientific consensus on the destruction of the environment with our self-forgetting, our rejection of who we are as creatures of a loving Creator, living inside His creation but at odds with it. It's the sadness of a humanity rich in know-how but lacking the inner security of knowing ourselves as creatures of God's love, a knowledge expressed in our simultaneous respect for God, for each other, and for creation. To talk about creation, you need poetry and beauty.' Pope Francis, *Let Us Dream* (London: Simon and Schuster UK, 2020), 33.

64. André Louf, *The Cistercian Way* (Kalamazoo: Cistercian Publications, 1983), 73. Trappist monk, André Louf (1929–2010) was one of the great

While common conversation about prayer generally talks about how *we* pray, the truth about prayer is that prayer is much more something God does in us, rather than something we do for God. 'We do not know how to pray,' says Saint Paul, so 'the Spirit intercedes for us with cries too deep for words' (Rom 8:26). Prayer is something that is happening in the person from the moment our life begins. As we grow in prayer throughout our lives, we become more and more present to God. This is the mystery to which André Louf refers: long before people are aware of it, or before one might take interest in it, God is praying ceaselessly within the person – within every person.

Prayer, then, is more a matter of awakening to what is going on within us than any new initiative on our part. In many ways, prayer is a response: it is a response to the God who dwells within us, it is the Holy Spirit who is poured into our hearts, crying 'Abba! Father!', as Paul told the early Christians in Galatia (see Gal 4:6). Pope Saint John Paul II captured it thus:

> In every authentic religious experience, the most characteristic expression is prayer. Because of the human spirit's constitutive openness to God's action of urging it to self-transcendence, we can hold that 'every authentic prayer is called forth by the Holy Spirit, who is mysteriously present in the heart of every person'.[65]

As well as a response to what happens within us, prayer is also a response to what happens to us: to moments or situations of fear or loss, to moments of indescribable joy as in the birth of a child or in the fulfilment of a long-awaited dream. Prayer is also the response to the beauty and power of creation: to a huge harvest moon, to a warm sunset, to the stillness of a snow-covered landscape, to the power – and threat – of a storm. The Bible is filled with accounts of such responses: we remember the story of the Calming of the Storm where the disciples, in a raging

---

masters of prayer in the Western tradition during the last quarter of the twentieth century and in the early years of the current century.

65. Pope Saint John Paul II in the General Audience of 9 September 1998, citing his address to the members of the Roman Curia of 22 December 1986. In that audience, the Holy Father was addressing what Christians have in common with people who are religious in other faiths, in whom we are called to 'recognize "the seeds of the Word" present and active' (see *Ad Gentes*, 11; *Lumen Gentium*, 17).

storm with a sleeping Jesus in a sinking boat, 'wake him up and say to him, "Teacher, do you not care that we are perishing?"' And he calms the storm, 'and they are filled with great awe' (Mark 4:35–41). While this is a story about the storms of life, it is also a story about the awesome power of nature and its capacity to bring us to the limits of who and what we are.

6.1.2 Prayer in the Face of Creation's Power, Awe and Beauty[66]

Among the many Old Testament stories that recount the meetings of people with God, one in particular stands out because of the way it captures the interplay of nature's power, God's mystery and our response. The story, from 1 Kings, is of Elijah's encounter with God on Mount Horeb. The heart of the story is as follows:

> The Word of the Lord came to Elijah and said, 'Go out and stand on the mountain before the Lord, for the Lord is about to pass by.' Now there was a great wind, so strong that it was splitting mountains and breaking rocks in pieces before the Lord, but the Lord was not in the wind; and after the wind an earthquake, but the Lord was not in the earthquake; and after the earthquake a fire, but the Lord was not in the fire; and after the fire a sound of sheer silence. When Elijah heard it, he wrapped his face in his mantle and went out and stood at the entrance of the cave. Then there came a voice to him that said, 'What are you doing here, Elijah?'
>
> (1 Kings 19:11–13; NRSV)

In a way, one could say that this story describes Elijah's experience of God. How God comes to him is not as Elijah expects. There is a mighty wind that signals the presence of God, 'but the Lord was *not in the wind*'. This is followed by an

66. When confronted with phenomena greater than ourselves, silence is a natural and healthy response. Our silence expresses that we are creatures, and embodies the realisation that we possess no ultimate power. Water possessed more than symbolic power for the ancients: it had the potential to enable life and to destroy it utterly, leading to its role in the renewal of the earth in the 'Great Flood' of Genesis 6–9. The terrifying power of water and fire is seen with ever-increasing frequency in the extreme weather events of recent years.

earthquake, 'but the Lord was *not in the earthquake*'. And the earthquake was followed by fire, 'but the Lord was *not in the fire*'.

It is not in the manifestation of God's power that God is to be met, but in what follows. The power of nature stops us in our tracks, but the mystery of God is something beyond. The response of Elijah tells us a great deal. He realises where God is not. In the face of mystery, he covers his face. He covers his face and waits. In his waiting, a voice comes to him.

There are two parts: the recognising and the waiting. This is the heart of what we can do. God will come to us in God's own time. An important part of prayer is waiting: waiting for God to speak, waiting for God to show God's hand, waiting for God to reveal his presence. To wait in hope is a key expression of faith. Life-giving faith is much more about waiting in hope for God to reveal himself than it is about signing up to a set of beliefs we feel we are asked to accept. The Church is the community of people who wait together 'in joyful hope for the coming of our Lord and Saviour', as we pray in the Mass. The Lord comes not only at the end of our lives and at the end of time, but the Lord comes – during our lives – to those who wait. The Church as community of faith supports us in our waiting and, guided by the Holy Spirit, the living Tradition helps us recognise for ourselves the signs of the Lord's presence in what unfolds in our hearts and in what unfolds in our lives.[67] The Lord of Creation is the living God (see Matt 16:16) who bring us to life (see Gal 3:21), and who sustains all life (see Mark 12:27).

The interplay between creation, the person, and the Creator is dynamic and ongoing. All three are interwoven: the manifestation of God's power and beauty in nature, the opening of our eyes and ears, and God's unique word to us in the intimacy of our hearts. The cosmic in all its vastness and the personal in all its intimacy are woven together in the one outreach of the Creator to all that he has made. Our response, indeed our call,

---

67. In Catholic theology, Tradition is the living self-communication of God. Tradition is the faith kept alive by the Spirit of Christ risen among his people. 'Tradition is an essentially social and ecclesial reality; its locus is the Church as a communion. It is transmitted not only by written and spoken words but equally by prayer, sacramental worship and participation in the Church's life.' Avery Dulles in the foreword to Yves Congar, *The Meaning of Tradition* (San Francisco: Ignatius Press, 2004).

is to be a place where the mystery of God can unfold. Where God brought Elijah is where God brings all who turn to him.

Once again we turn to the Psalms, Israel's prayer book, as it is called, and the prayer book of Jesus, Mary and Joseph. In Psalm 77, we discover the psalmist finding new words for ancient truths. Recalling the Hebrews' terrifying journey out of slavery in Egypt, the psalmist weaves his awe-filled experience of creation into a prayer of confidence and trust in the face of the faithfulness of the unknowable God:

> The waters saw you, O God,
> the waters saw you and trembled;
> the depths were moved with terror.
> The clouds poured down rain,
> the skies sent forth their voice;
> your arrows flashed to and fro.
> Your thunder rolled round the sky,
> your flashes lighted up the world.
> The earth was moved and trembled
> when your way led through the sea,
> your path through the mighty waters
> and no one saw your footprints.
> You guided your people like a flock
> by the hand of Moses and Aaron.   (Ps 77:16–20)

God does wondrous things but erases his 'footprints'. We cannot 'see' what God is doing, but those who are attentive can come to know God's care, God's providence, and the stirrings of the Lord in their midst.

6.1.3 Our Prayer and Creation: Praying with Creation

> Perhaps this is because in nature we come face to face with God's creation. It's not a movie or a painting or a church hymn, made by a human being, that is moving us, it's something that God ... created.[68]

68. James Martin SJ, 'How to Pray with Nature', *America* (2 September 2019), www.americamagazine.org/faith/2019/09/03/how-pray-nature.

The words we use in prayer reveal our most fundamental experiences and beliefs. It is probably in the Book of Psalms above all that we come across the response of people to the prayer that rises in reflection and wonder at the power of the Creator as it is revealed in creation. The religious and poetic imagination of the Psalms is profoundly cosmic. The resultant poetry and prayer are immersed in creation, and bring out the revelatory character of the richness and diversity of the natural world for all who spend time with them.

> The Lord hurls down hailstones like crumbs.
> The waters are frozen at God's touch;
> he sends forth his word and it melts them:
> at the breath of his mouth the waters flow.   (Ps 147:17–18)

The Psalms confront their hearers and readers with the cosmic power of God. The limits of the literal combined with the concreteness of the imagery increase the sensitivity of those who spend time with the Psalms to the sacredness of what God has made, and bring their readers along the road of gratitude, blessing and praise.[69]

The Scriptures are filled with examples of prayerful response to creation's variety, abundance, richness, power and force. In Psalm 35 the psalmist gives thanks to the One who is the source of life and light.

---

69. Authentic prayer witnesses variety: while petition and intercession are key dimensions of prayer, prayer is more than petition. Prayer is more than asking. The person who is fully alive, and who brings God into the variety of their life, will see their prayer grow and develop. Reflecting life, prayer will, over time, bring to expression praise, thanksgiving, blessing, but also remorse, sorrow, and lament. God does not write with straight lines, but reveals the grace of his presence, the mystery that we are, and the wonder of creation in the twists and turns that mark our existence. Growing in the love of God can mean giving up many of our childhood certainties. This is both liberation and loss. It demands simplicity and courage: the simplicity to grieve over what we have lost, and the courage to embrace the new life God puts before us. All of this – and more – is the business of prayer. 'When I was a child, I spoke like a child, I thought like a child, I reasoned like a child; when I became an adult, I put an end to childish ways ... Now, we see in a mirror, dimly, but then we will see face to face' (1 Cor 13:11–12).

Your love, Lord, reaches to heaven;
your truth to the skies.
Your justice is like God's mountain,
your judgments like the deep.
To both mortal and beast you give protection.
O Lord, how precious is your love.

My God, all your children
find refuge in the shelter of your wings.
They feast on the riches of your house;
they drink from the stream of your delight.
In you is the source of life
and in your light we see light.   (Ps 36:5–9)

We praise you, Father, with your Son
And Spirit blest,
In whom creation lives and moves,
And find its rest [70]

What the psalmist saw is also seen by the three young men in
the Book of Daniel. In their dire situation, their confidence in God
is expressed in a song of praise (Daniel 3:35–66) which calls on
everything that God has made to bless its creator: sun and moon,
showers and rain, breezes and winds, cold and heat, frost and snow.

And you, sun and moon, O bless the Lord.
And you, the stars of the heav'ns, O bless the Lord.
And you, showers and rain, O bless the Lord.
To him be highest glory and praise for ever.

And you, all you breezes and winds, O bless the Lord.
And you, fire and heat, O bless the Lord.
And you, cold and heat, O bless the Lord.
To him be highest glory and praise for ever. [71]

The same prayer can be ours when our eyes are opened to the
wonders of nature that surrounds us. The prayers of the Bible,

70. This doxology, or prayer of praise, comes from the Church's practice of ending the prayer of the Psalms with an expression of praise to the Creator – Father, Son, and Spirit.

71. The full text of this canticle may be found in Appendix 1.

especially the Psalms and canticles, are the school of our own prayer. In them we learn to walk in the ways of thanksgiving and praise. When, like children, who need the support of another before walking alone, so too walking in prayer with the canticles and Psalms, there comes the day when we make our own song of praise. Like Saint Francis, we are given the words for our own canticle of creation.

6.1.4 Prayer for Creation, Prayer for the Earth, Prayer for All God's Creatures

In prayer people express their awe and gratitude towards God, and in prayer we also express our deepest need. When we pray we bring to God that which is bigger than ourselves, and over which we have no control.

There are many aspects of creation that we bring to our Heavenly Father in prayer. The following strike me as worthy of attention in our prayer of intercession.

In responding to the cry of the earth, we might, over and over again, pray for the following:

for people ...	because this crisis comes from people and profoundly affects people's lives;
for change in ecological awareness and sensitivity ...	because the world needs people with a new heart, a new energy, and a new set of priorities;
for justice in all its dimensions, for the cry of the poor ...	because a lasting solution must be a solution which embraces all, includes all, and benefits all;
for scientists ...	since technological and scientific responses are an important part of the way forward;
for artists and musicians and poets ...	because the world needs their vision, their passion, their imagination, their realism and hope;

for people of faith ...   that we may realise that we do not save ourselves, but need the generosity and endurance which God gives.

I put before you the advice of Abbot John Chapman that the only way to pray is to pray, and that the prayer we make, even if it seems unsatisfactory, is of more value than the 'perfect' prayer we never make.

> [T]he only way to pray is to pray; and the way to pray is to pray much. If one has no time for this, then one must at least pray regularly. But the less one prays, the worse it goes.[72]

The Christian is a person who follows Jesus. As we pray we follow Christ into prayer. All through his life, Jesus turned to his Father in prayer, bringing to him the deepest needs of his own heart, and of the world. In the face of the environmental crisis and all its challenges, we do well to turn to our Father and intercede for the earth. May we have a love of the earth and a love of our sisters and brothers that will permit us to pray to our Father without ceasing (see 1 Thess 5:16–18).

6.2 Community as Ground and Empowerment for Another Way of Living

> The great temptation during a time of crisis is to retreat to what we consider a safe space. In fact, what we most need is to go out of our comfort zones and accompany one another, even when that calls for effort and even some risk.[73]

The climate crisis is a societal issue. Addressing it – nationally and globally – requires a societal response. One aspect of this is the response of communities, and *Church is profoundly about community*. Jesus called his disciples to follow him, not as a collection of individuals, but as people involved with others in a shared mission. Peter and Andrew, James

72. Abbot John Chapman (1865–1933), 'Letter XII (To One Living in the World)'. See Abbot Chapman, *Spiritual Letters* (London: Sheed and Ward, 1935; reprint London: Continuum, 2003), 52–3.

73. See Cardinal Blase Cupich, 'Letter on Violence in Chicago', Archdiocese of Chicago, 9 July 2021. Accessed 14 July 2021, www.archchicago.org/en/statement/-/article/2021/07/09/cardinal-cupich-on-violence-in-chicago.

and John were called together (see Mark 1:16–19), and the disciples were sent out in mission two by two (see Luke 10:1). While there is an essential personal dimension to everyone's Christian vocation, the call to discipleship comes out of community, and is directed towards community. We are a community of disciples, a community of people who follow Jesus. Community is formed by those in it, and acts through their action. It is intensely and profoundly a 'people' entity, and requires leadership and inspiration. Both leadership and inspiration are non-linear: they come from the most surprising of places. Who would have imagined that a Swedish teenager would make such a difference? But she has, and wonderfully so. One can equally marvel at the contribution of women religious to the climate debate and the ensuing transformation of the Church's climate response in many parts of the world. Young or old, deeply involved in the life of the Church or beyond, everyone can make a difference.

Confronted with the crisis of the man who was set upon by the robbers, the Samaritan *acts*. This is what sets him apart. He gets involved; he takes a risk; he invests in the one whose life hangs in the balance. The life of our planet hangs in the balance. The response must be one of action, but effective action demands reflection, focus and direction. Action for action's sake is futile, more an expression of despair than the embodiment of hope.

What do we need to do as individuals and communities? We need to change. The Church – locally and globally – needs to become even more an agent of change. Rather than seeking to reinvent the wheel, one might turn to the *Laudato Si'* Action Platform (www.laudatosiactionplatform.org). Among the many worthy proposals and initiatives, I would like to highlight the following:

- Adopting sustainable lifestyles
- Parish *Laudato Si'* groups
- Local ecology: rootedness and belonging in local communities
- Developing and deepening an ecological spirituality
- Raising awareness and promoting biodiversity
- Welcome and respect for the vulnerable, particularly those driven from their homelands by natural disasters, famine, and war

This focused list does not preclude other types of action that may be deemed more necessary, or more appropriate, in particular local situations, or for the skills of a particular group. What we need to keep before us is that without a community response, there is absolutely no hope of addressing the climate crisis. While individuals can make a very decisive contribution, it is only a community response that will make a palpable difference to the future of our common home.

6.2.1 *Laudato Si'* and your Parish: Practical Steps

> I've learnt that no one is too small to make a difference. And if a few children can get headlines all over the world just by not going to school – then imagine what we all could do together if we really wanted to.
>
> (Greta Thunberg)[74]

The purpose of this pastoral letter is to initiate a diocesan conversation about how all can contribute to the care of our common home and recognise the many dimensions attached to this challenge. We are at a critical moment as a global community and so I wish to encourage all people of faith to embark on this journey to live our call to protect and care for the garden of the world.

To that end I invite parishes throughout the archdiocese first of all to celebrate the Season of Creation each year from 1 September to 4 October (Feast of St Francis of Assisi). The Season of Creation could be a springboard for parish communities to embrace a spirituality that recovers a religious vision of God's creation and encourages greater contact with the natural world. I encourage all parishes in the diocese to appoint a *Laudato Si'* advocate who might lead a parish-based 'Care for Creation' group. I suggest that the issue of a Church response to the ecological crisis be placed regularly on the agenda of Parish Pastoral Council meetings. Unless our response to the ecological crisis is on the Parish Pastoral Council agenda at regular intervals, nothing will change. We have to bear in mind that the world has changed, and that the Church, like the Samaritan, is called to be proactive. Without embedding care for creation in the structures

74. Greta Thunberg, *No One Is Too Small to Make a Difference* (London: Penguin, 2019), 14.

of our diocese and of our parishes, our good intentions will not result in change.

In addition to parishes, I wish to invite Catholic schools in the diocese, primary and post-primary, to let their mission statements be inspired by *Laudato Si'*. In addition, catechists and religious education teachers might evaluate the role of an ecological spirituality in religious education programmes. I also invite all religious communities to be part of this diocesan discussion. I am conscious that many parishes, Catholic schools and religious congregations are already doing creative work around *Laudato Si'* through the leadership of Trócaire and other groups. I wish to endorse and encourage the initiatives already undertaken. Faith groups have a distinctive contribution to make in promoting another way of living by their witness, by the imaginative initiatives they support.

Parishes, schools and religious congregations are part of the one Christian family committed to the care of our common home. Together we can make a difference. As people of faith, we begin where we are on the journey; there is nowhere else we can begin. Embracing small actions can have a ripple effect across our different communities. In the words of Pope Francis, 'Everyone's talents and involvement are needed' so that 'all of us can cooperate as instruments of God for the care of creation' (*LS*, 14).

The need for action cannot be emphasised enough. People's good intentions and their talents must be united in common purpose. In the follow-up to *Laudato Si'*, Pope Francis called for communities to 'continue weaving networks so that the local churches may respond with determination to the cry of the earth and the cry of the poor'.[75] It is worth noting the elements of his call:

First, it is a call to communities;
second, it is a call to undertake something that will take
    time;
third, it is an undertaking will require skill, creativity,
    vision, and leadership;
fourth, it is not something static, but something dynamic;

75. Pope Francis, Words of Greeting to the Global Catholic Climate Movement at the General Audience of 1 February 2017.

fifth, it is about our common home *and* about the poor;
not either/or, but both/and; we fool ourselves if we think
that we can address the climate crisis without addressing
questions of justice and fairness.

My sisters and brothers, a culture by definition is a shared
reality. Christians, like the Lord Jesus himself, are both shaped
by and shape their culture. A culture of care calls us to be active
in weaving the networks that will make a difference. As the
Gaelic proverb says, *Ar scáth a chéile a mhaireann na daoine*
– 'In each other's shadow do we live', and also in each other's
light. Let parishes reach out to each other and to others: discover
common cause, act with common purpose, for the sake of the
common good. Parishes have all sorts of resources: spaces for
meetings, grounds for gardens, experience of working together,
communication networks, schools, a common identity, people
who are generous, ways of raising funds, and the list could go on.
Put those resources at the service of change, and at the service
of the poor. My experience as a priest in parish ministry has
brought home to me what communities are capable of, and what
together communities can give. You know how generously the
people of the Archdiocese of Dublin respond to the cry of the
poor. Think of the difference the people of the archdiocese –
with its large network of parishes – could make in responding
to the cry of the earth!

Authentic faith ... always involves a deep desire to change
the world, to transmit values, to leave this earth somehow
better than we found it.

(Pope Francis, *Evangelii Gaudium*, 183)

6.2.2 Hope in a World that has Changed, and for a Church that needs to Change

On a personal note, I wish to express my thanks to the many
women and men, who both as individuals and groups, have
inspired this pastoral, who have brought home its necessity and
urgency, and who continue to work for justice and the integrity
of creation. Many of you are people of deep faith; others among

you would not see yourselves in a religious perspective. In the struggle to reorder our priorities, our differences cannot be allowed to stand in the way. On the urgent journey to establishing a sustainable and equitable way of life for all, we have to travel together. The only road is the road forward; a longing for a world that was – frequently an idealised vision of the past – will not help. Glancing backwards with nostalgia will not empower change. There is no blueprint: as the Spanish poem so insightfully puts it, 'The road is made by walking.'[76]

6.3 Investing for Change: The *Laudato Si' Prize*

To underline the seriousness of what confronts us, to foster an imaginative response, and to stimulate change, the Archdiocese of Dublin is initiating the *Laudato Si' Prize*. This prize of €5,000 will be awarded for the new initiative that makes the greatest practical difference to our response to the climate crisis and to our embrace of the way of justice. People invest in what is important to them. The Samaritan gave a significant amount of money to the innkeeper: the wounded man had become his concern. Our common home concerns us all, and the Church has a responsibility of leadership. Through the *Laudato Si' Prize* the Church is investing in the healing of our common home, and in our shared future. While rooted in history, Christian faith proclaims that the failures, betrayals, and injustices of the past are not God's final word. God has raised his son from death, and his victory over death is a sign of God's faithfulness, and of God's call to follow his son.

The *Laudato Si' Prize* is in the service of healing our common home. It is, therefore, open to schools and community projects from all faiths and none. We are in this together. As explored in this pastoral letter, the God of the Christian is Father of all and Lord of all.

The fund for this prize is due to the generosity, hope and trust of the donors who have pledged to this initiative. I am grateful to them. An independent panel, the details of which will be announced in due course, will judge the prize.

---

76. From the poem, 'Caminante, No Hay Camino' by Spanish poet, Antonio Machado (1875–1939), where he says, *Caminante, no hay camino, se hace camino al andar!* ('Traveller, there is no road! The road is made by walking!')

Conclusion

In his poem, 'Begin', Brendan Kennelly, captures the paradoxical mystery-filled longings of the human heart.

> Though we live in a world that dreams of ending
> that always seems about to give in
> something that will not acknowledge conclusion
> insists that we forever begin.[77]

What Kennelly names resonates profoundly with the heart of Jesus' concern for his disciples:

> Do not be afraid, little flock, for it is your Father's good pleasure to give you the kingdom. Sell your possessions, and give alms. Make purses for yourselves that do not wear out ... For where your treasure is, there your heart will be also. Be dressed for action and have your lamps lit.
>
> (Luke 12:32–5)

Among the greatest dangers of the climate crisis are the loss of hope and the inaction that follows in its wake. Such a response represents a deep loss of faith, a withdrawal from the life God gives us, and is the death knell for our planet as we know it. Does the Risen Lord still not call us to a courageous response? Is 'be not afraid, little flock' not still his call?

The crisis is deep and vast. It is truly a global crisis that no single nation is able to tackle on its own. Paradoxically, because it is so vast and so omnipresent, it is difficult to grasp. 'Climate is an overarching, underlying condition of our lives and planet, and the change was incremental and intricate and hard to recognize if you weren't keeping track of this species or that temperature record.'[78] Such a deep crisis defies easy solutions (see *LS*, 171). There is no magic bullet.[79] That is not to say that – even now – we are condemned to inaction.

77. Cited in Niall MacMonagle (ed.), *Windharp: Poems of Ireland since 1916* (London: Penguin Ireland, 2015), 166. Originally in Brendan Kennelly, *Familiar Strangers: New & Selected Poems 1960–2004* (Hexham: Bloodaxe Books, 2004).
78. Rebecca Solnit, 'Our Climate Change Turning Point is Right Here, Right Now', *The Guardian*, 12 July 2021, www.theguardian.com/commentisfree/2021/jul/12/our-climate-change-turning-point-is-right-here-right-now.
79. 'As citizens of the 21st century, we have inherited an almighty mess,

Human beings have always been confronted by their insignificance before the vastness of the universe, and their powerlessness in the face of nature's power (see Psalm 98:7–9).[80] This has often been the context in which God has revealed to mortals our true role in the universe and in God's design. At this time, our God asks us to respond decisively and with urgency to the cry of the earth. That means, as parishes, groups, individuals, we have to figure out what will make a real difference and act to implement it. This pastoral letter has sketched many contours of what is involved. More will, no doubt, be rightly sketched by others. It is vital that we act. This is the bottom line.

We do not lose sight of the fact that we are people of faith. 'For people of faith, no matter the severity of the crisis, the last word is trust in God.' While faith 'does not give us ready-made solutions to complex problems', it does offer the consolation that, in trusting God, 'we can move forward'.[81] Therefore, this pastoral letter is also a call to hope. Hope is not a flight from painful reality, but the fruit of living faith. It provides the ultimate framework within which people can come to decisions and take action. 'Hope is not prognostication. It is an orientation of the spirit, an orientation of the heart; it transcends the world that is immediately experienced, and is anchored somewhere

---

but we have also inherited a lot of tools that could help us and others survive. A star among these tools – sparkling alongside solar panels, heat pumps, policy systems and activist groups – is modern climate science. It really wasn't all that long ago that our ancestors simply looked at air and thought it was just that – thin air – rather than an array of different chemicals; chemicals that you breathe in or out, that you might set fire to or could get high on, or that might, over several centuries of burning fossil fuels, have a warming effect on the earth. When climate fear starts to grip, it is worth remembering that we have knowledge that offers us a chance to act. We could, all too easily, be sitting around thinking: "The weather's a bit

weird today. Again." Alice Bell in *The Guardian*, 6 July 2021. Citing an extract from her book, *Our Biggest Experiment: An Epic History of the Climate Crisis* (London: Bloomsbury, 2021).

80. Let the sea and all within it, thunder;
the world, and all its peoples.
Let the rivers clap their hands
and the hills ring out their joy.
Rejoice at the presence of the Lord: for he comes
he comes to rule the earth.
(Psalm 98:7–9)

81. See Cardinal Blase Cupich, 'Letter on Violence in Chicago', Archdoicese of Chicago, 9 July 2021, accessed 14 July 2021, www.archchicago.org/en/statement/-/article/2021/07/09/cardinal-cupich-on-violence-in-chicago.

beyond its horizons.'[82] Ultimately, hope is a gift 'from elsewhere'. Like all gifts, it has to be received; it has to be welcomed.

Without a spirituality to sustain it, transformative hope will not endure. In this context it will be a spirituality that 'proposes an alternative understanding of the quality of life and encourages a prophetic and contemplative lifestyle ... marked by moderation and the capacity to be happy with [less]' (*LS*, 222). This is a truly Christian spirituality. It sustains the embodiment of hope in action; its measure is not what it receives but what it gives. It will also be an ecological spirituality, one which is born of a commitment to change and inclusion, and which sees the interrelatedness of all. It is a profound spirituality of community that takes seriously the finite character of all the earth's resources. The Christian will always remember that even on the cross, Jesus does not lose hope. Even when he feels abandoned, Jesus turns to his Father. This is not an easy word, but it is the word that is heard in the cry of the earth, the cry of the poor, and the cry of our Lord.

In particular, I wish to address a word to the young people of the Archdiocese of Dublin. What Pope Francis said at the 2013 World Youth Day in Rio de Janeiro about the mission of the Church,[83] I say to the youth of Dublin about the environment:

'*Hacen lío*! Make a fuss!' Make a fuss about the environment. Do not let us off the hook! We may not like to hear it. It will make us uncomfortable, but for your sakes and for ours, and for the sake of the poor and those who are oppressed, *call* us to account, *demand* action, *insist* on change.

---

82. Václav Havel, *Disturbing the Peace* (New York: Vintage, 1991), 181.
83. 'What do I expect as a result of this World Youth Day? I expect a fuss (*lío*). That here in Rio there will be fuss ... there will be, that here in Rio there will be drama ... There will be, but I want fuss in the dioceses, I want the Church to go out, I want the Church to go out into the streets, I want us to defend ourselves from everything that is worldly, from everything that is a "fixture", from everything that is comfort, from everything that is clericalism, from everything that is being closed in on ourselves, the parishes, the schools, the institutions – all are there in order to go out! If they do not go out, they become an NGO and the Church cannot be an NGO!' Address at World Youth Day, Cathedral of St Stephen, Rio de Janeiro, 25 July 2013.

This pastoral letter has been inspired by the leadership and vision of Pope Francis, and by his response to the situation of our world and all its inhabitants (see Psalm 24:1). To him I give the last word. May the Lord help us answer the call of this time.

> In the heart of this world,
> the Lord of life, who loves us so much, is always present.
> He does not abandon us, he does not leave us alone,
> for he has united himself definitively to our earth,
> and his love constantly impels us to find new ways forward.
> *Praise be to him!* (LS, 245)

Epilogue: A Word from the First Letter of Saint John

The climate catastrophe calls us to engage with environmental issues with an unprecedented urgency. It also challenges us to engage with the sources of our faith in new ways. We might take to heart the following reading of Saint John by Karl Löning and the late Erich Zenger. For them, the witness of God's word is 'that God never gives up on creation because God loves it, desires to inspire and alter the way we deal with creation'

> Those who say, 'I love God,'
>> and hate their sister the earth
>> are liars;
> For those who do not love their sister whom they have seen,
>> cannot love God whom they have not seen ...
>> those who love God
>> must love their sister, the earth, also. (See 1 John 4:20–1)[84]

Appendices

Appendix 1: Passages from the Bible for Prayer

The Parable of the Good Samaritan (Luke 10:25–37)
A parable is a story or an image that, by its freshness and vividness, teases its audience into active reflection. Jesus constantly used parables in his teaching to bring people to see the world and

---

84. From the closing lines of Karl Löning and Erich Zenger, *To Begin with, God Created: Biblical Theologies of Creation* (Collegeville: Liturgical Press, 2000), 190.

each other in new ways, bringing his hearers into a new order of perception and experience altogether. In his son, God is doing the 'new thing' of which Isaiah spoke (see Isaiah 43:19). Jesus' life puts flesh on his teaching; he himself is the embodiment of the parables.

A lawyer stood up to test Jesus. 'Teacher,' he said, 'what must I do to inherit eternal life?' Jesus said to him, 'What is written in the law? What do you read there?' He answered, 'You shall love the Lord your God with all your heart, and with all your soul, and with all your strength, and with all your mind; and your neighbour as yourself.' And he said to him, 'You have given the right answer; do this, and you will live.'

But wanting to justify himself, he asked Jesus, 'And who is my neighbour?' Jesus replied, 'A man was going down from Jerusalem to Jericho, and fell into the hands of robbers, who stripped him, beat him, and went away, leaving him half dead. Now by chance a priest was going down that road; and when he saw him, he passed by on the other side. So likewise a Levite, when he came to the place and saw him, passed by on the other side. But a Samaritan while travelling came near him; and when he saw him, he was moved with pity. He went to him and bandaged his wounds, having poured oil and wine on them. Then he put him on his own animal, brought him to an inn, and took care of him. The next day he took out two *denarii*, gave them to the innkeeper, and said, "Take care of him; and when I come back, I will repay you whatever more you spend."[85] Which of these three, do you think, was a neighbour to the man who fell into the hands of the robbers?' He said, 'The one who showed him mercy.' Jesus said to him, 'Go and do likewise.' (NRSV)

The Song of the Three Young Men (Daniel 3:35–66)[86]
O all you works of the Lord, O bless the Lord.
To him be highest glory and praise for ever.

85. A denarius is commonly reckoned as a day's wage for a labourer; about €150 in the Ireland of today. By giving two denarii, the Samaritan implies that he will return on the third day.

86. *The Song of the Three Young Men* is found in the Greek version of the Book of Daniel. The Greek version of the Jewish Bible, frequently referred to as the Septuagint, was the text of the Bible used by those Jews who left the Holy Land and settled throughout the Greek and Roman empires in the centuries after Alexander's conquest in 332 BCE. As Christianity initially blossomed among Greek-speaking Jewish communities of the ancient world, the Septuagint became the Church's first Bible.

And you, angels of the Lord, O bless the Lord.
To him be highest glory and praise for ever.
And you, the heavens of the Lord, O bless the Lord.
And you, clouds of the sky, O bless the Lord.
And you, all armies of the Lord, O bless the Lord.
To him be highest glory and praise for ever.

And you, sun and moon, O bless the Lord.
And you, the stars of the heav'ns, O bless the Lord.
And you, showers and rain, O bless the Lord.
To him be highest glory and praise for ever.

And you, all you breezes and winds, O bless the Lord.
And you, fire and heat, O bless the Lord.
And you, cold and heat, O bless the Lord.
To him be highest glory and praise for ever.

And you, showers and dew, O bless the Lord.
And you, frosts and cold, O bless the Lord.
And you, frost and snow, O bless the Lord.
To him be highest glory and praise for ever.

And you, night-time and day, O bless the Lord.
And you, darkness and light, O bless the Lord.
And you, lightning and clouds, O bless the Lord.

O let the earth bless the Lord.
To him be highest glory and praise for ever.

And you, mountains and hills, O bless the Lord.
And you, all plants of the earth, O bless the Lord.
And you, fountains and springs, O bless the Lord.
To him be highest glory and praise for ever.

And you, rivers and seas, O bless the Lord.
And you, creatures of the sea, O bless the Lord.
And you, every bird in the sky, O bless the Lord.
And you, wild beasts and tame, O bless the Lord.
To him be highest glory and praise for ever.

And you, children of men, O bless the Lord.
  To him be highest glory and praise for ever.
O Israel, bless the Lord. O bless the Lord.
  And you, priests of the Lord, O bless the Lord.
And you, servants of the Lord, O bless the Lord.
  To him be highest glory and praise for ever.
And you, spirits and souls of the just, O bless the Lord.
  And you, holy and humble of heart, O bless the Lord.
Ananias, Azarias, Mizael, O bless the Lord.
  To him be highest glory and praise for ever.

Let us praise the Father, the Son, and Holy Spirit:
  To you be highest glory and praise for ever.
May you be blessed, O Lord, in the heavens.
  To you be highest glory and praise for ever.[87]

Appendix 2: Poems for Reflection and Prayer

God's Grandeur Gerard Manley Hopkins SJ (1844–89)
The world is charged with the grandeur of God.
  It will flame out, like shining from shook foil;
  It gathers to a greatness, like the ooze of oil
Crushed. Why do men then now not reck his rod?
Generations have trod, have trod, have trod;
  And all is seared with trade; bleared, smeared with toil;
  And wears man's smudge and shares man's smell: the soil
Is bare now, nor can foot feel, being shod.

And for all this, nature is never spent;
  There lives the dearest freshness deep down things;
And though the last lights off the black West went,
  Oh, morning, at the brown brink eastward, springs —
Because the Holy Ghost over the bent
  World broods with warm breast and with ah! bright wings.

O Light Invisible TS Eliot (1888–1965)
O Light Invisible, we praise Thee!
Too bright for mortal vision.

87. The doxology, or prayer of praise, comes from the Church's practice of ending the prayer of the Psalms with an expression of praise to the Creator – Father, Son, and Spirit.

O Greater Light, we praise Thee for the less;
The eastern light our spires touch at morning,
The light that slants upon our western doors at evening,
The twilight over stagnant pools at batflight,
Moon light and star light, owl and moth light,
Glow-worm glowlight on a grassblade.
O Light Invisible, we worship Thee!

We thank Thee for the light that we have kindled,
The light of altar and of sanctuary;
Small lights of those who meditate at midnight
And lights directed through the coloured panes of
windows
And light reflected from the polished stone,
The gilded carven wood, the coloured fresco.
Our gaze is submarine, our eyes look upward
And see the light that fractures through unquiet water.
We see the light but see not whence it comes.
O Light Invisible, we glorify Thee!

Prayer to Saint Kevin of Glondalough

A Chaoimhín le caoineas do mhéine
Fuair an-chion ainmhithe is éanluith;
I do láthair ba ghnáth leo go léir a bheith
Gan scá romhat I bhfásach an fhéir ghlais.
Bímisne, a Chaoimhín na féile,
Dea-iompair le dúile gan éirim:
Dia a chruthaigh is a chuir ar an soal iad
Is cúiteoidh Sé linn an croí truamhéile.

Kevin, with your kind nature,
you were loved by animals and birds;
they stayed in your presence
without fear in the green grassy growth.
Let us all, o generous Kevin,
behave well towards dumb creatures:
God created them and put them into this world
and he will reward us for a merciful heart.[88]

88. Donla uí Bhraonáin (ed.), *Paidreacha na Gaeilge: Prayers in Irish* (Dublin:
Cois Life, 2009), 122–3.

Published 2021 by Veritas Publications
7–8 Lower Abbey Street, Dublin 1, Ireland
publications@veritas.ie
www.veritas.ie

ISBN 978-1-80097-020-5

Copyright © Archdiocese of Dublin, 2021

10 9 8 7 6 5 4 3 2

Cover photo: https://www.colorado.edu/
ecenter/2020/11/27/great-pacific-garbage-patch
All other photos: ©istockphoto.com

Printed in Ireland by Walsh Colour Print, Kerry

*Veritas books are printed on paper made from
the wood pulp of managed forests. For every
tree felled, at least one tree is planted, thereby
renewing natural resources.*